Welcom

Welcome to "The 5-Ingredient Gourmet", a delightful collection of easy yet flavorful dishes that celebrates the beauty of simplicity in cooking. As an artist and a food lover, I've always believed that food, like art, has the power to bring people together, spark joy, and nourish the soul. This cookbook is inspired by my love for creating beautiful moments—whether it's through painting, sharing a meal with loved ones, or exploring new flavors on my travels.

As a busy woman I know the value of meals that are both effortless and delicious. You'll find recipes here that are simple to make, but full of vibrant flavors, perfect for sharing with family and friends. Whether you're preparing breakfast on a quiet morning or whipping up dinner after a long day, these dishes will bring a little beauty and warmth into your kitchen. So grab your apron, explore new tastes, and let's create some beautiful memories—one simple, flavorful dish at a time!
Happy cooking!

Sincerely Yours, *Kateryna Piatakova*

TABLE OF CONTENTS

Dinner Time

Desserts Time

- "Begin your day with a peaceful heart; as you prepare your breakfast, let each step be a moment of calm. The way you start your morning sets the tone for the day—nourish your body and soul with kindness."

- "As you stir your breakfast ingredients, stir in a little joy. Cooking is a gentle reminder that you have control over how you shape your day. Let your kitchen be a sanctuary of warmth and positivity."

- "Greet the morning with a smile, and let your breakfast be a joyful start to your day, full of simple pleasures. As you prepare your meal, take a deep breath and savor the process—this is your time to center yourself and set a peaceful rhythm for the day ahead."

Breakfast
Time

Avocado Toast

INGREDIENTS

- 1 ripe avocado (approximately 150g)
- 2 slices whole grain bread (each slice approximately 30g)
- 1 tablespoon lemon juice (about 15ml)
- 1/4 teaspoon salt (about 1.5g)
- 1/4 teaspoon red pepper flakes (about 0.5g)

Optional: poached or fried eggs, tomatoes red bell pepper

DIRECTIONS

1. **Toast the bread slices:** Place the slices of whole grain bread in a toaster and toast until golden brown and crispy. This usually takes about 2-3 minutes, depending on your toaster's settings.
2. **Prepare the avocado mash:**
   - Cut the avocado in half and remove the pit.
   - Scoop the flesh into a bowl.
   - Add the lemon juice and salt to the avocado.
   - Use a fork to mash the avocado until smooth, leaving a few chunks for texture if desired.
3. **Assemble the avocado toast:**
   - Spread the mashed avocado evenly over the toasted bread slices.
   - Sprinkle the red pepper flakes on top for a bit of heat.
   - Optional: top with poached or fried eggs, tomatoes, red bell pepper.
4. **Serve:** Enjoy immediately as a quick and nutritious breakfast, snack, or light meal.

Avocado:
The avocado contributes most of the healthy fats, fiber, and calories. It's rich in monounsaturated fats, which are heart-healthy.

Whole Grain Bread:
Provides carbohydrates, fiber, and a small amount of protein. Whole grains are more nutritious and filling than refined grains.

Lemon Juice:
Adds flavor with minimal calories. It also helps prevent the avocado from browning.

Salt:
Enhances flavor, but it's important to use in moderation to manage sodium intake.

Red Pepper Flakes:
Add a spicy kick with negligible calories.

Nutritional Information (Per Serving): Calories: 315 kcal, Total Fat: 21g, Carbohydrates: 29g, Protein: 6g

"Start your day with a simple slice of goodness—every bite of avocado toast is a step toward nourishing yourself with love!"

Serving Suggestions:

- For extra protein, you can top the avocado toast with a poached or fried egg.
- Add sliced tomatoes, radishes, or cucumbers for added texture and nutrients.
- Drizzle with a little olive oil or balsamic glaze for extra flavor.

NOTES _____

Greek Yogurt Parfait

INGREDIENTS

- 2 cups Greek yogurt (approx. 480g)
- 4 tablespoons honey (approx. 60g)
- 1 cup granola (approx. 100g)
- 1 cup fresh berries (approx. 150g, mix of strawberries, blueberries, or raspberries)
- 4 tablespoons sliced almonds (approx. 28g)

Optional: nuts, nut butter

DIRECTIONS

1. **Prepare the ingredients:**
   - Measure out the Greek yogurt, honey, granola, fresh berries, and sliced almonds.
   - If using large berries, like strawberries, chop them into smaller pieces.
   - Experiment with different types of fruit or berries.
2. **Layer the parfait:**
   - In each of the two serving glasses or bowls, spoon 1/2 cup of Greek yogurt as the first layer.
   - Drizzle 1 tablespoon of honey over the yogurt in each glass.
   - Add 1/4 cup of granola on top of the yogurt and honey.
   - Layer 1/4 cup of fresh berries over the granola.
   - Repeat the layering with the remaining Greek yogurt, honey, granola, and berries.
   - Optional: add nuts and/or nut butter on top of Greek yogurt.
3. **Top with almonds:**
   - Sprinkle 2 tablespoons of sliced almonds on top of the final layer of berries in each serving glass.
4. **Serve immediately:** The parfaits are ready to be enjoyed right away, offering a perfect combination of creamy, sweet, and crunchy textures.

Greek Yogurt: A rich source of protein and calcium. It's lower in sugar compared to regular yogurt and helps keep you full longer due to its high protein content.

Honey: Adds natural sweetness to the parfait. Honey is a source of simple carbohydrates and provides a quick energy boost. It's also rich in antioxidants.

Granola: Contributes crunch and a hearty texture. Granola typically provides a mix of carbohydrates, healthy fats, and some protein. It's important to choose a variety low in added sugars.

Fresh Berries: Berries add natural sweetness, a burst of flavor, and vibrant color. They are packed with vitamins, antioxidants, and fiber, making them a nutrient-dense choice.

Sliced Almonds: Almonds provide a satisfying crunch, along with healthy fats, protein, and fiber. They are also a good source of vitamin E, magnesium, and antioxidants.

Nutritional Information (Per Serving) Calories: 480 kcal, Total Fat: 18g, Carbohydrates: 62g, Protein: 19g

"Layer up the joy with a Greek yogurt parfait—each spoonful is a sweet reminder to take care of yourself with kindness!"

Serving Suggestions:

- Serve as a quick, nutritious breakfast option, pairing it with a cup of coffee or tea.
- Use as a healthier alternative to traditional desserts, offering a balance of sweetness and creaminess.
- Experiment with different types of fruit, nuts, or even a drizzle of nut butter to add variety to your parfait.

NOTES _____

Spinach and Feta Omelette

 2 servings 15 minutes

INGREDIENTS

- 4 large eggs (approx. 200g)
- 1 cup fresh spinach, chopped (approx. 30g)
- 1/4 cup feta cheese, crumbled (approx. 40g) (or shredded cheese you like)
- 1 tablespoon olive oil (approx. 15ml)
- 1/4 teaspoon salt (approx. 1.5g)

Optional: bacon or ham bites

DIRECTIONS

1. **Prepare the Ingredients:** Wash (in cool water) and chop the spinach. Crumble the feta cheese and set aside.
2. **Heat the Skillet:** In a non-stick skillet, heat 1 tablespoon of olive oil over medium heat.
3. **Whisk the Eggs:** In a bowl, whisk the 4 large eggs with 1/4 teaspoon of salt until fully combined.
4. **Cook the Eggs:** Pour the whisked eggs into the skillet. Allow the eggs to cook undisturbed for about 1-2 minutes, or until they start to set around the edges.
5. **Add Spinach and Feta:** Evenly distribute the chopped spinach and crumbled feta cheese over the eggs.
- Optional: add bacon or ham bites for extra protein.
6. **Finish Cooking:** Cook for an additional 2-3 minutes, or until the eggs are fully set and the spinach is wilted.
7. **Fold the Omelette:** Carefully fold the omelette in half using a spatula. Cook for another minute if necessary to ensure the inside is fully cooked.
8. **Serve:** Slide the omelette onto a plate and serve immediately.

Eggs: Provide a substantial amount of high-quality protein, healthy fats, and various vitamins and minerals, including vitamin D and choline.

Spinach: Adds fiber, vitamins (notably vitamin K and A), and a small number of carbohydrates. It's low in calories and rich in antioxidants.

Feta Cheese: Contributes to the overall fat and protein content while adding a tangy flavor. It also provides calcium and sodium.

Olive Oil: Provides healthy monounsaturated fats and contributes to the omelette's overall richness. It also helps prevent the eggs from sticking to the skillet.

Salt: Enhances the flavor of the dish but should be used moderately to manage sodium intake.

Nutritional Information (Per Serving): Calories: 290 kcal, Total Fat: ~24g, Carbohydrates: ~3g, Protein: ~17g

"Whisk up some goodness with a spinach and feta omelette—it's a simple, delicious way to fuel your day with a touch of care and flavor!"

Serving Suggestions:
- Pair the omelette with a slice of whole-grain toast for additional fiber and carbohydrates.
- Serve alongside fresh fruit like berries or orange slices for a balanced and colorful meal.
- A simple side salad of mixed greens, tomatoes, and cucumbers dressed with a light vinaigrette complements the richness of the omelette.

NOTES _____

Berry Smoothie

 2 servings   8 minutes

INGREDIENTS

- 1 cup mixed berries (fresh or frozen) (approx. 150g)
- 1/2 cup Greek yogurt (approx. 120g)
- 1 tablespoon honey (approx. 15g)
- 1 cup spinach (approx. 30g)
- 1 cup almond milk (approx. 240ml)

Optional: nut butter

DIRECTIONS

1. **Add all ingredients:**
- Add mixed berries (strawberries, raspberries, blueberries), Greek yogurt, honey, spinach, and almond milk—into a blender.
- Experiment with different types of fruit or berries.
- Experiment with different types of milk.
- Optional: add nut butter for extra flavor.
2. **Blend** until the mixture is smooth and creamy.
3. **Pour** into glasses and serve chilled.

Mixed Berries: Provide natural sweetness, vitamins, antioxidants, and fiber, contributing to the carbohydrate content.

Greek Yogurt: Adds creaminess and a good amount of protein, also contributing to the total fat and some carbohydrates.

Honey: Acts as a natural sweetener, adding carbohydrates and a slight boost in calories.

Spinach: Adds a nutritional boost without significantly altering the flavor, contributing to vitamins, minerals, and fiber with minimal calories.

Almond Milk: A dairy-free alternative that adds a subtle nutty flavor and helps blend the smoothie, contributing to a small amount of fat and calcium.

Nutritional Information (Per Serving): Calories: 290 kcal, Total Fat: ~24g, Carbohydrates: ~3g, Protein: ~17g

"Blend your way to a brighter day with a berry smoothie—every sip is a refreshing reminder to nourish yourself with love and positivity!"

Serving Suggestions:
- Add a tablespoon of chia seeds or flax seeds for extra fiber and omega-3 fatty acids.
- Pair the smoothie with a slice of whole-grain toast topped with avocado for a balanced meal.
- Use frozen berries or add a few ice cubes to achieve a thicker, more refreshing consistency.

NOTES _____

Banana Oat Pancakes

  2 servings   15 minutes

INGREDIENTS

- 2 ripe bananas (approx. 240g)
- 1 cup oats (approx. 90g)
- 2 large eggs (approx. 100g)
- 1/2 teaspoon vanilla extract (approx. 2.5ml)
- 1 teaspoon baking powder (approx. 4g)

Optional: olive oil for cooking

DIRECTIONS

1. **Mash the Bananas:** In a medium bowl, mash the ripe bananas until smooth.
2. **Mix the Ingredients:** Add oats, eggs, vanilla extract, and baking powder to the mashed bananas. Stir until the mixture is well combined.
3. **Cook the Pancakes:** Heat a non-stick skillet over medium heat. Pour about 1/4 cup of the batter onto the skillet for each pancake. Cook for 2-3 minutes, or until bubbles form on the surface, then flip and cook for another 2-3 minutes until golden brown. Optional: if you don't have non-stick skillet use an olive oil for cooking.
4. **Serve:** Serve warm with your favorite toppings like fresh berries, honey, or a dollop of yogurt.

Bananas: Provide natural sweetness, potassium, and fiber. They also contribute to the moisture and binding of the pancakes.

Oats: Offer complex carbohydrates, fiber, and a small amount of protein, making the pancakes filling and hearty.

Eggs: Add protein, structure, and richness to the pancakes.

Vanilla Extract: Enhances flavor without adding extra calories.

Baking Powder: Acts as a leavening agent, helping the pancakes rise and become fluffy.

Nutritional Information (Per Serving): Calories: 370 kcal, Total Fat: 10g, Carbohydrates: 55g, Protein: 14g

"Flip into a great day with banana oat pancakes—each bite is a warm hug of wholesome goodness to start your morning right!"

Serving Suggestions:

- Top with a drizzle of honey, a handful of fresh berries, or a spoonful of nut butter for added flavor and nutrition.
- Serve with a side of Greek yogurt for extra protein.

NOTES _____

Banana Chia Overnight Oats

 2 servings   5 minutes +

INGREDIENTS

- 1 cup rolled oats (approx. 90g)
- 1 medium banana, mashed (approx. 120g)
- 2 tablespoons chia seeds (approx. 30g)
- 1 cup almond milk (approx. 240ml)
- 1/2 teaspoon vanilla extract

Optional: 1 tablespoon honey (optional, for sweetness), Banana slices for garnish (optional)

DIRECTIONS

1. **Mash the Bananas:** In a medium bowl, mash the ripe bananas until smooth.
2. **Mix Ingredients:** In a medium bowl or jar, combine the rolled oats, mashed banana, chia seeds, almond milk, honey (if using), and vanilla extract. Stir well until all the ingredients are evenly distributed.
3. **Refrigerate:** Cover the bowl or jar and refrigerate overnight (or for at least 4 hours). The oats and chia seeds will absorb the liquid, and the mixture will thicken.
4. **Stir and Serve:** In the morning, give the oats a good stir. Add a little more almond milk if the consistency is too thick for your liking. Top with fresh banana slices for garnish if desired.

Banana: Adds natural sweetness and creaminess, along with potassium and vitamins.

Rolled Oats: Provide complex carbohydrates, fiber, and protein, giving this breakfast its hearty base and long-lasting energy.

Chia Seeds: These little seeds are packed with omega-3 fatty acids, fiber, and protein. They help thicken the oats and provide a nutritional boost.

Almond Milk: A plant-based milk that adds creaminess with fewer calories than traditional dairy milk.

Vanilla Extract: Enhances the flavor with a subtle sweetness and aroma.

Nutritional Information (Per Serving): Calories: 320 kcal, Total Fat: 8g, Carbohydrates: 56g, Protein: 8g

"Wake up to the wholesome goodness of banana chia overnight oats—creamy, nourishing, and packed with flavor to fuel your day right from the start!"

Serving Suggestions:
- Toppings: Try adding chopped nuts, seeds, or additional fruit like blueberries or strawberries for texture and flavor variety.
- Make Ahead: This recipe is perfect for meal prep. Make a few servings at once and store them in individual containers for a quick, healthy breakfast throughout the week.
- Customizations: Feel free to swap almond milk with any other milk (cow's milk, coconut milk, etc.) or add spices like cinnamon for extra warmth.

NOTES _____

Cheese and Ham Breakfast Wrap

  2 servings   🕐 12 minutes

INGREDIENTS

- 2 whole wheat tortillas (approx. 60g each)
- 4 slices of ham (approx. 120g total)
- 1/2 cup shredded cheese (approx. 50g, cheddar or your choice)
- 2 large eggs (approx. 100g total)
- 1/2 cup fresh spinach (approx. 15g)

Optional: salt and pepper to taste

DIRECTIONS

1. **Scramble the Eggs:** In a non-stick skillet, scramble the eggs over medium heat until fully cooked. Add salt and pepper to taste. Set aside.
2. **Assemble the Wraps:** Lay out the tortillas. Place 2 slices of ham on each tortilla, followed by half of the scrambled eggs, 1/4 cup of shredded cheese, and 1/4 cup of spinach on each.
3. **Roll and Heat:** Roll up the tortillas tightly, folding in the sides as you go. Heat the wraps in the skillet over medium heat for 2-3 minutes on each side, or until the cheese melts and the tortillas are slightly crispy.
4. **Serve:** Slice in half and serve immediately.

Whole Wheat Tortillas: Provides complex carbohydrates and fiber, making the wrap more filling and nutritious than using white tortillas.

Ham: A good source of protein, with some fat. Opt for lean ham to reduce the fat content.

Shredded Cheese: Adds richness and creaminess, along with protein and fat. Choose a low-fat option to reduce calories.

Eggs: Packed with high-quality protein and healthy fats, eggs are a staple breakfast ingredient.

Fresh Spinach: Adds a dose of vitamins, minerals, and fiber with minimal calories.

Nutritional Information (Per Serving): Calories: 400 kcal, Total Fat: 20g, Carbohydrates: 28g, Protein: 25g

"Wrap up your morning with a cheesy ham delight—quick, comforting, and a delicious way to fuel your day with a smile!"

- Pair the wrap with a side of fresh fruit or a small green salad for a balanced meal.
- For extra flavor, add a dollop of salsa or hot sauce inside the wrap before rolling.

NOTES

Mushroom and Chive Scrambled Eggs

 2 servings   15 minutes

INGREDIENTS

- 4 large eggs (approx. 200g)
- 1/2 cup mushrooms, sliced (approx. 60g)
- 2 tablespoons fresh chives, chopped (approx. 6g)
- 1 tablespoon butter (approx. 14g)
- 1/4 teaspoon salt (approx. 1.5g)

Optional: black pepper, parsley

DIRECTIONS

1. Heat a skillet over medium heat and melt the butter.
2. Add the sliced mushrooms and sauté until tender, about 4-5 minutes.
3. In a bowl, whisk together the eggs and salt. Optional: add black pepper to taste.
4. Pour the egg mixture into the skillet with the mushrooms.
5. Stir gently and continuously until the eggs are scrambled and fully cooked, about 3-4 minutes.
6. Remove from heat and sprinkle with chopped chives or/and parsley before serving.

Eggs: The eggs are the primary source of protein and healthy fats, providing essential vitamins like B12 and D.

Mushrooms: Add a savory, umami flavor and contribute fiber, vitamins, and minerals such as selenium and potassium.

Chives: Offer a mild onion-like flavor and are rich in vitamins A and C, along with antioxidants.

Butter: Provides richness and enhances the flavor while adding to the total fat content.

Salt: Enhances the overall taste, but should be used in moderation to manage sodium intake.

Nutritional Information (Per Serving): Calories: 248 kcal, Total Fat: 20g, Carbohydrates: 4g, Protein: 14g

"Stir up some flavor with mushroom and chive scrambled eggs—simple, savory, and the perfect way to brighten your morning with care!"

Serving Suggestions:

- Serve the scrambled eggs with whole-grain toast or a side of fresh fruit for a balanced breakfast.
- Pair with a small glass of orange juice or a cup of coffee to complement the flavors.
- Add a sprinkle of black pepper or a dash of hot sauce for an extra kick.

NOTES _____

Tomato Basil Breakfast Sandwich

 2 servings   10 minutes

INGREDIENTS

- 4 slices whole grain bread (approx. 120g)
- 1 tomato, sliced (approx. 120g)
- 4 fresh basil leaves
- 2 slices mozzarella cheese (approx. 60g)
- 1 tablespoon olive oil (approx. 15ml)

Optional: pepper to taste

DIRECTIONS

1. Drizzle olive oil on both slices of bread.
2. Lightly toast the bread until golden brown.
3. Layer one slice of toasted bread with mozzarella cheese, tomato slices, and fresh basil leaves. Optional: add pepper to taste if desired.
4. Top with the other slice of bread to form a sandwich.
5. Optional: make it warm in microwave oven.
6. Serve immediately.

Whole Grain Bread: Provides complex carbohydrates, fiber, and some protein. Whole grains help with sustained energy release.

Tomato: Adds freshness, moisture, and a boost of vitamins A and C with minimal calories.

Basil Leaves: Contribute a fragrant flavor with negligible calories and are rich in antioxidants.

Mozzarella Cheese: Provides protein and calcium but also contributes to the total fat content.

Olive Oil: Adds healthy monounsaturated fats and enhances the flavor of the sandwich.

Nutritional Information (Per Serving): Calories: 335 kcal, Total Fat: 21g, Carbohydrates: 25g, Protein: 12g

"Take a bite of freshness with a tomato basil breakfast sandwich—crisp, flavorful, and a tasty way to start your day with a smile!"

Serving Suggestions:
- Serve the sandwich with a side of mixed greens or a fruit salad for a complete breakfast.
- Pair with a cup of coffee or fresh orange juice to balance the meal.

NOTES _____

Fruit Salad

 2 servings   10 minutes

INGREDIENTS

- 1 cup strawberries, hulled and halved (approx. 150g)
- 1 cup blueberries (approx. 150g)
- 1 kiwi, peeled and sliced (approx. 100g)
- 1 banana, sliced (approx. 100g)
- 1 tablespoon honey (approx. 15g)

Optional: cream, ice-cream, Greek yogurt, nuts, granola

DIRECTIONS

1. In a large bowl, combine strawberries, blueberries, kiwi, and banana.
2. Drizzle with honey and gently toss to coat the fruit evenly.
3. Experiment with different types of fruit.
4. Optional: top with cream, ice-cream, Greek yogurt, nuts or granola if desired.
5. Serve immediately or chill in the refrigerator for 15-30 minutes before serving.

Strawberries: Provide a good source of Vitamin C, fiber, and antioxidants, with a low calorie count.

Blueberries: Rich in antioxidants, Vitamin C, and Vitamin K, adding natural sweetness to the salad.

Kiwi: Offers Vitamin C, Vitamin K, and fiber, contributing to the tartness and color of the salad.

Banana: Adds potassium, Vitamin B6, and natural sweetness, making the salad more filling.

Honey: A natural sweetener that enhances the flavor while adding minimal fat.

Nutritional Information (Per Serving): Calories: 182 kcal, Total Fat: 1g, Carbohydrates: 45g, Protein: 2g

"Brighten your day with a colorful fruit salad—each bite is a sweet reminder to nourish your body with nature's best!"

NOTES _____

Shakshuka

 2 servings   20 minutes

INGREDIENTS

- 4 large eggs (approx. 200g)
- 1 can (14 oz/400g) of crushed tomatoes
- 1 red bell pepper, diced (approx. 120g)
- 1 small onion, diced (approx. 70g)
- 2 tablespoons olive oil (approx. 30ml)

Optional: fresh parsley, pepper to taste

DIRECTIONS

1. **Prepare the Base:**
Heat olive oil in a large skillet over medium heat. Add the diced onion and red bell pepper. Sauté for about 5-7 minutes until the vegetables are softened.

2. **Cook the Tomatoes:**
Pour in the crushed tomatoes, stirring well to combine with the vegetables. Simmer the mixture for about 10 minutes, allowing it to thicken slightly.

3. **Add the Eggs:**
Make four small wells in the tomato mixture using the back of a spoon. Crack an egg into each well. Cover the skillet and cook for about 5-7 minutes until the eggs are set to your liking.

4. **Serve:**
Remove from heat and serve the Shakshuka directly from the skillet. Optional: sprinkle with fresh parsley and/or pepper if desired.

Eggs: Provide protein and healthy fats, making them the primary source of protein in this dish.

Crushed Tomatoes: Offer a rich source of vitamins A and C, as well as lycopene, which is an antioxidant.

Red Bell Pepper: Adds a sweet, slightly tangy flavor and is packed with vitamins, particularly vitamin C.

Onion: Enhances the flavor profile of the dish with a slight sweetness as it caramelizes.

Olive Oil: Provides healthy monounsaturated fats, contributing to the richness of the dish.

Nutritional Information (Per Serving): Calories: 320 kcal, Total Fat: 21g, Carbohydrates: 18g, Protein: 15g

"Spice up your morning with a warm, flavorful shakshuka—each bite is a comforting reminder that simple ingredients can create something extraordinary!"

Serving Suggestions:
- Serve the Shakshuka with crusty bread to soak up the delicious tomato sauce.
- Add a sprinkle of fresh herbs like parsley or cilantro for extra flavor.
- Pair with a side salad for a more complete meal.

NOTES _____

- "While your soup simmers, let your thoughts settle into a peaceful rhythm. The slow, gentle process of cooking is a reminder to take life one step at a time —nourish yourself with patience and peace."

- "Stirring a pot of soup is like stirring a pot of comfort. Let the warmth of the kitchen wrap around you, and as the flavors meld together, let your worries dissolve into the rhythm of your day."

- "Cooking soup is an act of self-care; each ingredient you add is a step toward creating something nourishing and heartfelt. As you prepare your meal, take a moment to breathe deeply and fill your heart with gratitude for the simple joys in life."

Soup

Time

Tomato Basil Soup

 2 servings   25 minutes

INGREDIENTS

- 1 can (14.5 oz/400g) of tomatoes
- 1/4 cup fresh basil leaves (approx. 10g)
- 1/4 cup onion, chopped (approx. 30g)
- 1 clove garlic, minced (approx. 3g)
- 1 tablespoon olive oil (approx. 15ml)

Optional: cream, pepper to taste

DIRECTIONS

1. **Sauté Onions and Garlic:**
   - Heat olive oil in a medium-sized pot over medium heat.
   - Add the chopped onions and sauté for about 3-5 minutes until they become translucent.
   - Add the minced garlic and sauté for another 1-2 minutes until fragrant.
2. **Simmer Tomatoes:**
   - Pour in the canned tomatoes, including the juice, and stir to combine with the onions and garlic.
   - Reduce the heat to low and let the mixture simmer for about 15 minutes, allowing the flavors to meld together.
3. **Blend the Soup:**
   - Remove the pot from heat and add the fresh basil leaves.
   - Use an immersion blender to blend the soup until smooth. Alternatively, you can carefully transfer the soup to a blender and blend in batches.
4. **Serve:**
   - Once the soup is smooth and creamy, return it to the pot and heat through if needed.
   - Serve hot, garnished with additional basil leaves, dollop of cream and sprinkle with pepper if desired.

Canned Tomatoes: The base of the soup, providing a rich source of vitamins C and A, as well as lycopene, an antioxidant known for its potential health benefits.

Fresh Basil Leaves: Add a fragrant, fresh flavor and contribute to the soup's overall taste and aroma.

Onion: Adds depth and sweetness to the soup, complementing the acidity of the tomatoes.

Garlic: Enhances the flavor with its aromatic qualities, giving the soup a savory undertone.

Olive Oil: Used to sauté the onions and garlic, it adds a touch of healthy fat and richness to the soup.

Nutritional Information (Per Serving): Calories: 130 kcal, Total Fat: 7g, Carbohydrates: 15g, Protein: 2g

"Savor the warmth of tomato basil soup—a comforting bowl of goodness that nourishes your body and lifts your spirits!"

Serving Suggestions:
- Serve the Tomato Basil Soup with a side of crusty bread for dipping.
- Top with a drizzle of olive oil or a dollop of cream for added richness.
- Pair with a simple grilled cheese sandwich for a classic comfort meal.

NOTES _____

Vegetable Broth

 2 servings   35 minutes

INGREDIENTS

- 1 carrot, peeled and chopped (approx. 50g)
- 1 celery stalk, chopped (approx. 40g)
- 1/2 onion, chopped (approx. 40g)
- 1 garlic clove, smashed (approx. 5g)
- 4 cups water (approx. 960ml)

Optional: Salt and pepper to taste

DIRECTIONS

1. **Prepare the Ingredients:**
- Peel and chop the carrot.
- Chop the celery stalk and onion.
- Smash the garlic clove with the side of a knife to release its flavor.

2. **Cook the Vegetables:**
- In a medium-sized pot, add the chopped carrot, celery, onion, and smashed garlic.
- Pour in 4 cups of water.

3. **Simmer the Broth:**
- Bring the mixture to a boil over medium-high heat.
- Once it reaches a boil, reduce the heat to low and let it simmer for about 30 minutes.
- Occasionally skim off any foam or impurities that rise to the surface.

4. **Strain and Use the Broth:**
- After simmering, strain the broth through a fine mesh sieve or cheesecloth to remove the solids.
- Optional: season with salt and pepper if desired.

5. **Use or Store:** Use the broth immediately in your recipe, or let it cool to room temperature before storing it in the refrigerator for up to 3 days or freezing it for later use.

Carrot: Provides a natural sweetness and depth to the broth, contributing flavor and a small amount of vitamins and minerals.

Celery: Adds a mild, peppery flavor and is a classic base ingredient for broths, bringing a balance to the sweetness of the carrot.

Onion: Contributes a savory flavor and depth, enhancing the overall richness of the broth.

Garlic: Adds a subtle, aromatic depth and a hint of spiciness to the broth.

Water: Acts as the base, extracting flavors from the vegetables to create a light, aromatic broth.

Nutritional Information (Per Serving): Calories: 20 kcal, Total Fat: 0g, Carbohydrates: 5g, Protein: 0g

"Let the soothing warmth of vegetable broth fill your soul—simple, wholesome, and a gentle way to nourish your body with care!"

Serving Suggestions:
- Use this vegetable broth as a base for soups, stews, or risottos.
- Enjoy it as a light, warming drink, especially when seasoned with herbs and spices.
- It's an excellent vegetarian or vegan substitute for chicken broth in various recipes.

NOTES _____

Broccoli Cheddar Soup

 2 servings   20 minutes

INGREDIENTS

- 2 cups broccoli florets (fresh or frozen) (approx. 150g)
- 1 cup shredded cheddar cheese (approx. 100g)
- 1/4 cup onion, chopped (approx. 30g)
- 1 cup vegetable broth (approx. 240ml)
- 1/2 cup milk (approx. 120ml)

DIRECTIONS

1. **Cook Broccoli and Onion:**
   - In a medium pot, bring the vegetable broth to a simmer over medium heat.
   - Add the chopped onion and broccoli florets to the broth.
   - Cook for 10-12 minutes, or until the broccoli is tender and the onion is soft.
2. **Blend the Soup:**
   - Remove the pot from heat.
   - Use an immersion blender to blend the soup until smooth. Alternatively, transfer the soup to a blender and blend until smooth, then return to the pot.
3. **Add Milk and Cheese:**
   - Return the pot to low heat.
   - Stir in the milk and gradually add the shredded cheddar cheese, stirring constantly until the cheese is fully melted and the soup is creamy and smooth.
4. **Serve:**
   - Serve the soup hot, with a sprinkle of extra cheddar cheese or a dash of black pepper if desired.

Broccoli Florets: Provides the bulk of the soup, adding fiber, vitamins (especially C and K), and minerals like iron and potassium. Broccoli also gives the soup its vibrant green color.

Shredded Cheddar Cheese: Adds a rich, creamy texture and a sharp flavor to the soup, while also contributing protein and fat.

Onion: Adds a sweet, aromatic base to the soup, complementing the savory flavors of the broccoli and cheddar.

Vegetable Broth: Acts as the soup's base, enhancing the overall flavor while keeping the dish vegetarian.

Milk: Contributes creaminess and balances the sharpness of the cheddar cheese, making the soup smooth and velvety.

Nutritional Information (Per Serving): Calories: 290 kcal, Total Fat: 20g, Carbohydrates: 12g, Protein: 15g

"Cozy up with a bowl of broccoli cheddar soup—rich, creamy, and the perfect blend of comfort and nourishment to brighten your day!"

Serving Suggestions:
- Serve with a slice of crusty bread or a bread roll for dipping.
- Garnish with extra shredded cheddar cheese, a sprinkle of chives, or a dash of hot sauce for added flavor.
- Pair with a light salad for a more complete meal.

NOTES _____

Butternut Squash Soup

 2 servings 30 minutes

INGREDIENTS

- 2 cups butternut squash, peeled and cubed (approx. 300g)
- 1/4 cup onion, chopped (approx. 40g)
- 2 cups vegetable broth (approx. 480ml)
- 1/2 cup cream (approx. 120ml)
- 1/4 teaspoon nutmeg (approx. 0.5g)

DIRECTIONS

1. **Prepare the Ingredients:**
   - Peel and cube the butternut squash.
   - Chop the onion.
2. **Cook the Squash and Onion:**
   - In a medium-sized pot, combine the cubed butternut squash, chopped onion, and vegetable broth.
   - Bring the mixture to a boil over medium-high heat.
   - Reduce the heat to low, cover the pot, and let it simmer for about 15-20 minutes, or until the butternut squash is tender and easily pierced with a fork.
3. **Blend the Soup:**
   - Using an immersion blender, blend the soup directly in the pot until smooth. Alternatively, you can transfer the soup to a blender in batches and blend until smooth.
   - Return the blended soup to the pot if using a traditional blender.
4. **Add Cream and Nutmeg:**
   - Stir in the cream and add the nutmeg to the soup.
   - Cook over low heat for another 2-3 minutes, stirring occasionally, until the soup is heated through and the flavors are well combined.
5. **Serve:** Ladle the soup into bowls and serve hot. Garnish with a sprinkle of additional nutmeg, a swirl of cream, or some chopped fresh herbs if desired.

Butternut Squash: This is the star ingredient, providing a naturally sweet, nutty flavor. It's rich in vitamins A and C, fiber, and antioxidants, making the soup both flavorful and nutritious

Onion: Adds a mild, savory depth to the soup, balancing the sweetness of the squash.

Vegetable Broth: Acts as the liquid base, enhancing the soup's flavor with a savory, aromatic depth. Using a low-sodium broth can help control the soup's sodium content.

Cream: Introduces richness and a velvety texture to the soup, making it more indulgent. It also adds a good amount of fat, which makes the soup more satisfying.

Nutmeg: Provides a warm, slightly sweet spice that complements the natural sweetness of the butternut squash and adds complexity to the flavor.

Nutritional Information (Per Serving): Calories: 240 kcal, Total Fat: 14g, Carbohydrates: 26g, Protein: 3g

"Embrace the warmth of butternut squash soup—smooth, sweet, and a delicious reminder to savor the simple joys in every spoonful!"

Serving Suggestions:
- Serve the Butternut Squash Soup as a warming starter or as a main course with crusty bread or a side salad.
- For a gourmet touch, drizzle with a bit of olive oil or a swirl of cream on top, and sprinkle with toasted pumpkin seeds or fresh herbs like thyme or parsley.
- Pair it with a light sandwich or a fall-inspired salad featuring roasted nuts and apples to create a well-rounded meal.

NOTES _____

Chicken Broth

 2 servings   40 minutes

INGREDIENTS

- 1 chicken breast or 2 chicken thighs (approx. 200g)
- 4 cups water (approx. 960ml)
- 1 carrot, peeled and chopped (approx. 50g)
- 1 celery stalk, chopped (approx. 40g)
- 1/2 onion, chopped (approx. 40g)

Optional: Salt and pepper to taste

DIRECTIONS

1. **Prepare the Ingredients:**
   - Peel and chop the carrot.
   - Chop the celery stalk and onion.
   - If using chicken breast or thighs with skin, you can leave it on for extra flavor.
2. **Cook the Chicken and Vegetables:**
   - In a medium-sized pot, add the chicken, chopped carrot, celery, and onion.
   - Pour in 4 cups of water.
3. **Simmer the Broth:**
   - Bring the mixture to a boil over medium-high heat.
   - Once it reaches a boil, reduce the heat to low and let it simmer for about 30-40 minutes.
   - Occasionally skim off any foam or impurities that rise to the surface.
4. **Strain and Use the Broth:**
   - After simmering, remove the chicken and vegetables from the pot.
   - Strain the broth through a fine mesh sieve or cheesecloth to remove any remaining solids.
   - Optional: Season with salt and pepper if desired.
5. **Use or Store:** Use the broth immediately in your recipe, or let it cool to room temperature before storing it in the refrigerator for up to 3 days or freezing it for later use.

Chicken: The chicken provides the essential flavor base for the broth and contributes protein and a small amount of fat. Using bones (if available) enhances the richness and depth of flavor.

Carrot: Adds a natural sweetness and depth of flavor to the broth, balancing the savory notes.

Celery: Contributes a mild, slightly peppery flavor, which complements the other vegetables.

Onion: Adds a savory base, enhancing the broth's overall depth and complexity.

Water: The water extracts the flavors from the chicken and vegetables, turning into a rich, aromatic broth.

Nutritional Information (Per Serving): Calories: 50 kcal, Total Fat: 1g, Carbohydrates: 3g, Protein: 8g

"Warm your heart with a bowl of homemade chicken broth—a soothing elixir that nurtures both body and soul, reminding you to take care of yourself!"

Serving Suggestions:
- Use this chicken broth as a base for soups, stews, or sauces.
- Enjoy a warm cup of broth on its own for a light, nourishing snack.
- It pairs well with various dishes and can be seasoned with additional herbs and spices for extra flavor.

NOTES _____

Chicken Tortilla Soup

 2 servings 15 minutes

INGREDIENTS

- 1 cup cooked chicken, shredded (approx. 150g)
- 1 cup tortilla chips (approx. 50g)
- 1/2 cup salsa (approx. 120g)
- 2 cups chicken broth (approx. 480ml)
- 1/2 avocado, sliced (approx. 75g)

DIRECTIONS

1. **Heat the Broth and Salsa:**
- In a medium pot, combine the chicken broth and salsa.
- Bring to a simmer over medium heat.
2. **Add the Chicken:**
- Add the shredded cooked chicken to the pot.
- Reduce heat to low and simmer for about 10 minutes, allowing the flavors to meld together.
3. **Serve:**
- Ladle the soup into bowls.
- Top with tortilla chips and avocado slices just before serving to keep the chips crunchy.

Cooked Chicken: Provides lean protein, making the soup satisfying and nutritious. Shredded chicken adds texture and absorbs the flavors of the broth and salsa.

Tortilla Chips: Add a crunchy texture and a salty contrast to the soup's smooth broth. They can also be used as a thickening agent if stirred in.

Salsa: Serves as a flavorful base, adding spice, tomatoes, onions, and other vegetables to the soup with minimal effort.

Chicken Broth: Acts as the soup's base, enhancing the savory flavors and providing hydration and warmth.

Avocado: Adds a creamy, rich texture to balance the soup's spice and provides healthy monounsaturated fats.

Nutritional Information (Per Serving): Calories: 320 kcal, Total Fat: 18g, Carbohydrates: 22g, Protein: 20g

"Spice up your day with a bowl of chicken tortilla soup—each hearty spoonful is a delightful blend of flavors that warms your soul and lifts your spirits!"

Serving Suggestions:

- Garnish with shredded cheese, sour cream, or fresh cilantro for additional flavor and richness.
- Serve with lime wedges on the side to squeeze over the soup, adding brightness and acidity.
- Pair with a side of cornbread or a simple green salad for a more substantial meal.

NOTES _____

Chicken Noodle Soup

INGREDIENTS

- 1 cup cooked chicken breast, shredded (approx. 150g)
- 1 cup egg noodles (approx. 60g)
- 2 cups chicken broth (approx. 480ml)
- 1/2 cup carrots, sliced or cubed (approx. 60g)
- 1/4 cup celery, chopped (approx. 30g)

DIRECTIONS

1. **Prepare the Vegetables:**
- Slice or cube the carrots and chop the celery.
2. **Cook the Vegetables:**
- In a medium pot, bring the chicken broth to a boil.
- Add the sliced or cubed carrots and chopped celery to the broth.
- Reduce the heat to medium and simmer for about 10 minutes, or until the vegetables are tender.
3. **Add the Noodles:**
- Stir in the egg noodles and cook according to the package instructions, usually about 6-8 minutes, until they are tender.
4. **Add the Chicken:**
- Add the shredded cooked chicken to the pot and stir to combine.
- Simmer for an additional 2-3 minutes to heat the chicken through.
5. **Serve:** Ladle the soup into bowls and serve hot.

Chicken Breast: Provides lean protein, making the soup hearty and satisfying.

Egg Noodles: Add carbohydrates for energy, contributing to the soup's comfort-food appeal.

Chicken Broth: Forms the flavorful base of the soup, rich in minerals and adds depth to the dish.

Carrots: Contribute sweetness and are a good source of beta-carotene and fiber.

Celery: Adds a slight crunch and subtle flavor, along with fiber and vitamins.

Nutritional Information (Per Serving): Calories: 240 kcal, Total Fat: 5g, Carbohydrates: 25g, Protein: 22g

"Wrap yourself in comfort with a bowl of chicken noodle soup—every spoonful is a warm hug that nourishes your body and brings a smile to your heart!"

Serving Suggestions:
- Serve the chicken noodle soup with a side of crackers or a slice of crusty bread.
- Garnish with fresh parsley or a squeeze of lemon juice for added brightness.
- Pair with a light salad for a balanced and comforting meal.

NOTES _____

Cucumber Dill Soup

INGREDIENTS

- 1 cucumber, peeled and chopped (approx. 200g)
- 1 cup Greek yogurt (approx. 240g)
- 1 tablespoon fresh dill, chopped (approx. 2g)
- 1 clove garlic, minced (approx. 3g)
- 1 tablespoon lemon juice (approx. 15ml)

Optional: salt and pepper to taste

DIRECTIONS

1. **Prepare the Ingredients:**
- Peel and chop the cucumber.
- Mince the garlic.
- Chop the fresh dill.

2. **Blend the Soup:**
- In a blender, combine the chopped cucumber, Greek yogurt, chopped dill, minced garlic, and lemon juice.
- Optional: add salt and pepper to taste.
- Blend until smooth and creamy.

3. **Chill and Serve:**
- Transfer the blended soup to a bowl.
- Refrigerate for at least 30 minutes to allow the flavors to meld and the soup to chill.
- Serve cold, garnished with additional dill and sprinkle with black pepper if desired.

Cucumber: The cucumber serves as the base, providing a refreshing, hydrating quality to the soup. It's low in calories and rich in vitamins and antioxidants.

Greek Yogurt: Adds a creamy texture and a tangy flavor to the soup, as well as protein and probiotics, making the dish more filling and nutritious.

Fresh Dill: Offers a bright, herbaceous flavor that complements the cucumber and yogurt. Dill is also a good source of antioxidants.

Garlic: Adds a subtle, savory depth to the soup with its pungent flavor. Garlic is also known for its health benefits, including boosting the immune system.

Lemon Juice: Provides a zesty brightness and helps balance the richness of the yogurt, enhancing the overall flavor of the soup.

Nutritional Information (Per Serving): Calories: 110 kcal, Total Fat: 5g, Carbohydrates: 8g, Protein: 7g

"Refresh your senses with a chilled cucumber dill soup—crisp, creamy, and a delightful reminder to savor the lightness of summer in every spoonful!"

Serving Suggestions:
- Serve the Cucumber Dill Soup as a light and refreshing appetizer or a cool summer meal.
- Pair with a side of crusty bread or a simple salad for a more substantial lunch.
- For an added touch, garnish with a drizzle of olive oil or a few slices of cucumber on top.

NOTES _____

Gazpacho Soup

 2 servings   40 minutes

INGREDIENTS

- 3 medium ripe tomatoes, chopped (approx. 300g)
- 1/2 cucumber, peeled and chopped (approx. 100g)
- 1/4 red bell pepper, chopped (approx. 50g)
- 1 clove garlic, minced (approx. 3g)
- 1 tablespoon olive oil (approx. 15ml)

Optional: salt and pepper to taste

DIRECTIONS

1. **Prepare the Vegetables:**
- Chop the tomatoes, cucumber, and red bell pepper into small pieces.
- Mince the garlic.
2. **Blend the Ingredients:**
- In a blender, combine the chopped tomatoes, cucumber, red bell pepper, and minced garlic.
- Blend until smooth, adjusting the consistency by adding a little cold water if needed.
3. **Add Olive Oil:** With the blender running on low, slowly drizzle in the olive oil to emulsify the mixture and create a smooth texture.
4. **Chill the Soup:**
- Transfer the blended soup to a bowl or container.
- Refrigerate for at least 30 minutes before serving to allow the flavors to meld and the soup to chill thoroughly.
5. **Serve:**
- Stir the soup before serving, adjusting seasoning with salt and pepper if desired.
- Pour into bowls or glasses and serve cold.

Tomatoes: Provide the base for the soup, rich in vitamins A and C, and lycopene, an antioxidant that has numerous health benefits.

Cucumber: Adds a refreshing, hydrating element to the soup, contributing to its cooling effect.

Red Bell Pepper: Adds sweetness and a vibrant color to the soup, along with a dose of vitamin C.

Garlic: Infuses the soup with a robust, savory flavor, and has anti-inflammatory properties.

Olive Oil: Adds richness and depth to the soup, while also contributing heart-healthy monounsaturated fats.

Nutritional Information (Per Serving): Calories: 120 kcal, Total Fat: 7g, Carbohydrates: 13g, Protein: 2g

"Cool down with a vibrant bowl of gazpacho—bursting with fresh flavors, it's a delicious reminder to enjoy the taste of summer in every refreshing sip!"

Serving Suggestions:
- Serve the gazpacho cold as a refreshing starter or light meal, garnished with extra diced vegetables, croutons, or a drizzle of olive oil.
- Pair it with crusty bread or a side salad for a more filling meal.
- For a spicy kick, add a pinch of cayenne pepper or a dash of hot sauce before blending.

NOTES _____

Miso Soup

🍴 2 servings   🕐 10 minutes

INGREDIENTS

- 2 cups water (approx. 480ml)
- 2 tablespoons miso paste (red or white)
- 1/2 cup tofu, cubed (approx. 100g)
- 1/4 cup scallions, sliced (approx. 15g)
- 1/4 cup wakame seaweed, dried (approx. 5g)

DIRECTIONS

1. **Prepare the Ingredients:**
   - Cube the tofu into small, bite-sized pieces.
   - Slice the scallions thinly.
   - Rehydrate the dried wakame seaweed by soaking it in water for 5 minutes, then drain and set aside.
2. **Heat the Water:**
   - In a medium-sized pot, bring 2 cups of water to a gentle boil over medium heat.
3. **Add Tofu and Wakame:**
   - Once the water is boiling, reduce the heat to low and add the cubed tofu and rehydrated wakame.
   - Simmer for about 2-3 minutes.
4. **Dissolve the Miso Paste:**
   - Take a small amount of the hot broth from the pot and place it in a separate bowl.
   - Add the miso paste to the bowl and whisk until fully dissolved.
   - Return the dissolved miso mixture to the pot and stir gently. Do not let the soup boil after adding the miso, as it can affect the flavor and nutritional value.
5. **Finish with Scallions:** Add the sliced scallions to the pot, stirring briefly to combine.
6. Remove from heat and serve immediately.

Miso Paste: The star ingredient, miso paste provides a rich, umami flavor and is packed with probiotics, which are beneficial for gut health.

Tofu: Adds protein and a creamy texture to the soup, making it more filling and nutritious.

Scallions: Contribute a fresh, mild onion flavor that brightens up the soup and adds color.

Wakame Seaweed: Adds a subtle oceanic flavor and is rich in minerals like iodine and calcium, contributing to the soup's nutritional value.

Water: Forms the base of the soup, allowing the other ingredients to infuse and blend together.

Nutritional Information (Per Serving): Calories: 80 kcal, Total Fat: 4g, Carbohydrates: 8g, Protein: 6g

"Experience the comforting warmth of miso soup—each soothing bowl is a gentle reminder to nourish your spirit with simplicity and love!"

Serving Suggestions:

- Serve the miso soup as a starter or a light meal, accompanied by a side of rice or a small salad.
- For added richness, you can sprinkle some sesame seeds or drizzle a little sesame oil on top before serving.
- Pair it with sushi or other Japanese dishes for a complete meal.

NOTES _____

- "As you toss your salad, imagine you're tossing in a bit of sunshine. Each colorful ingredient is a reminder of the freshness and vitality that surrounds you—let your day be as crisp and refreshing as the meal you're creating."

- "Preparing a salad is like arranging a garden on your plate. Let the vibrant colors and textures inspire a sense of peace and creativity, and as you mix it all together, embrace the harmony that comes from nourishing both body and soul."

- "In every slice and chop, there's a moment to center yourself. As you prepare your salad, take in the crispness of the vegetables and the bright flavors— let this be a time to refresh your spirit and bring a little lightness to your day."

Salads
Time

Chicken Caesar Salad

 2 servings 🕐 20 minutes

INGREDIENTS

- 4 cups Romaine lettuce, chopped (approx. 200g)
- 1 cup grilled chicken breast, sliced (approx. 150g)
- 1/4 cup Caesar dressing (approx. 60ml)
- 1/4 cup Parmesan cheese, grated (approx. 20g)
- 1/2 cup croutons (approx. 30g)

DIRECTIONS

1. **Prepare the Lettuce:**
- Wash and chop the Romaine lettuce into bite-sized pieces.
- Pat the lettuce dry with a paper towel or use a salad spinner to remove excess moisture.

2. **Grill the Chicken:**
- If you haven't already grilled the chicken, season a chicken breast with salt and pepper and grill it over medium heat for about 6-8 minutes per side, or until fully cooked (internal temperature of 165°F/74°C).
- Let the chicken rest for a few minutes, then slice it into thin strips.

3. **Assemble the Salad:**
- In a large salad bowl, toss the chopped Romaine lettuce with the Caesar dressing until evenly coated.
- Top the dressed lettuce with the grilled chicken slices, grated Parmesan cheese, and croutons.

4. **Serve:** Divide the salad between two plates and serve immediately with a sprinkle of extra parmesan cheese if desired.

Romaine Lettuce: Provides a crisp, refreshing base that is low in calories but high in vitamins A and K.

Grilled Chicken: Adds lean protein, making the salad more filling and nutritious.

Caesar Dressing: Offers rich, creamy flavor and binds the salad together, though it is higher in fat.

Parmesan Cheese: Adds a salty, nutty flavor that complements the Caesar dressing and provides a source of calcium.

Croutons: Contribute a satisfying crunch and additional carbohydrates, balancing the texture of the salad.

Nutritional Information (Per Serving): Calories: 380 kcal, Total Fat: 25g, Carbohydrates: 10g, Protein: 28g

"Elevate your meal with a chicken Caesar salad—crisp, creamy, and a delicious way to treat yourself while staying balanced and nourished!"

Serving Suggestions:
- Serve the Chicken Caesar Salad as a light main course or as a side dish with a bowl of soup.
- Pair with a glass of iced tea or a light white wine like Pinot Grigio.
- For added flavor, sprinkle with freshly cracked black pepper or a squeeze of lemon juice.

NOTES _____

Greek Salad

INGREDIENTS

- 1 cucumber, sliced (approx. 200g)
- 1 cup cherry tomatoes, halved (approx. 150g)
- 1/2 cup Kalamata olives, pitted (approx. 75g)
- 1/2 cup feta cheese, crumbled (approx. 75g)
- 1/4 red onion, thinly sliced (approx. 50g)

Optional: Olive oil, Salt and pepper to taste

DIRECTIONS

1. **Prepare the Vegetables:**
- Slice the cucumber into thin rounds or half-moons.
- Halve the cherry tomatoes.
- Thinly slice the red onion.
- Pit the Kalamata olives if they are not already pitted.
2. **Assemble the Salad:**
- In a large salad bowl, combine the cucumber slices, halved cherry tomatoes, Kalamata olives, and sliced red onion.
- Gently toss the vegetables together.
3. **Add the Feta:**
- Crumble the feta cheese over the top of the salad.
- Gently mix the salad to distribute the feta evenly.
4. **Serve:** Divide the salad between two plates and serve immediately. Drizzle olive oil, salt and pepper to taste.

Cucumber: Adds a refreshing, hydrating crunch to the salad, with minimal calories.

Cherry Tomatoes: Provide sweetness and juiciness, along with vitamins A and C.

Kalamata Olives: Contribute a briny, salty flavor and healthy monounsaturated fats.

Feta Cheese: Offers a tangy, creamy texture that complements the other flavors, along with protein and calcium.

Red Onion: Adds a sharp, pungent flavor that contrasts nicely with the other ingredients.

Nutritional Information (Per Serving): Calories: 220 kcal, Total Fat: 18g, Carbohydrates: 10g, Protein: 5g

"Enjoy a burst of freshness with a Greek salad—colorful, crunchy, and a delightful way to nourish your body with vibrant flavors!"

Serving Suggestions:
- Serve the Greek Salad as a light lunch or as a side dish to grilled meats or fish.
- Pair with warm pita bread and a side of hummus for a complete Mediterranean meal.
- Drizzle with extra virgin olive oil and a splash of red wine vinegar for added flavor, if desired.

NOTES _____

Spinach and Strawberry Salad

 2 servings   10 minutes

INGREDIENTS

- 2 cups fresh spinach leaves (approx. 60g)
- 1/2 cup strawberries, sliced (approx. 75g)
- 1/4 cup feta cheese, crumbled (approx. 30g)
- 1/4 cup sliced almonds (approx. 25g)
- 2 tablespoons balsamic vinaigrette (approx. 30ml)

DIRECTIONS

1. **Prepare the Ingredients:**
- Wash and dry the spinach leaves.
- Slice the strawberries into thin slices.
- Crumble the feta cheese if it is not pre-crumbled.
- Lightly toast the sliced almonds in a dry skillet over medium heat for 2-3 minutes, until golden and fragrant. Allow them to cool.
2. **Assemble the Salad:**
- In a large salad bowl, add the spinach leaves.
- Top with sliced strawberries, crumbled feta cheese, and toasted almonds.
3. **Dress the Salad:**
- Drizzle the balsamic vinaigrette over the salad.
- Toss gently to ensure the dressing coats all the ingredients evenly.
4. **Serve:** Divide the salad between two plates and serve immediately.

Spinach Leaves: Provide a fresh, leafy base rich in vitamins A and C, as well as iron and antioxidants.

Strawberries: Add sweetness and a juicy texture, along with vitamin C and fiber.

Feta Cheese: Offers a tangy flavor that complements the sweetness of the strawberries, along with calcium and protein.

Sliced Almonds: Contribute a nutty crunch and healthy fats, as well as protein and fiber.

Balsamic Vinaigrette: Adds a balanced acidity and sweetness to tie the flavors together, with a modest calorie contribution.

Nutritional Information (Per Serving): Calories: 210 kcal, Total Fat: 15g, Carbohydrates: 12g, Protein: 5g

"Delight in a spinach and strawberry salad—each bite is a sweet and savory celebration of health that brightens your day with every forkful!"

Serving Suggestions:
- Serve the Spinach and Strawberry Salad as a light lunch or as a refreshing side dish to grilled chicken or fish.
- Pair with a crusty whole-grain baguette and a glass of white wine for a simple yet elegant meal.
- For added variety, consider adding a sprinkle of fresh basil leaves or a handful of blueberries.

NOTES _____

Caprese Salad

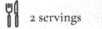 2 servings • 10 minutes

INGREDIENTS

- 2 medium tomatoes, sliced (approx. 200g)
- 1/2 cup fresh mozzarella, sliced (approx. 60g)
- 1/4 cup fresh basil leaves (approx. 10g)
- 1 tablespoon olive oil (approx. 15ml)
- 1 tablespoon balsamic reduction (approx. 15ml)

Optional: pepper to taste

DIRECTIONS

1. **Prepare the Ingredients:**
- Slice the tomatoes and fresh mozzarella into even rounds.
- Wash and dry the fresh basil leaves.
2. **Assemble the Salad:**
- On a serving plate, alternate slices of tomato and mozzarella in a circular pattern or in rows.
- Tuck fresh basil leaves between the tomato and mozzarella slices.
3. **Dress the Salad:**
- Drizzle the olive oil evenly over the tomato, mozzarella, and basil.
- Follow with the balsamic reduction, drizzling it artfully over the salad.
- Optional: sprinkle with black pepper if desired.
4. **Serve:** Serve the Caprese Salad immediately, either chilled or at room temperature.

Tomatoes: Provide juiciness and a slightly sweet, tangy flavor, rich in vitamins A and C, and antioxidants like lycopene.

Fresh Mozzarella: Offers a creamy texture and mild flavor, along with protein, calcium, and some healthy fats.

Fresh Basil Leaves: Add a fragrant aroma and fresh taste, along with antioxidants and essential vitamins.

Olive Oil: Contributes healthy monounsaturated fats and enhances the overall flavor profile of the salad.

Balsamic Reduction: Adds a sweet and tangy richness that balances the flavors, with minimal added calories.

Nutritional Information (Per Serving): Calories: 190 kcal, Total Fat: 15g, Carbohydrates: 7g, Protein: 7g

"Savor the simplicity of a Caprese salad—fresh, vibrant, and a delicious reminder to enjoy the beauty of good ingredients!"

NOTES _____

Cucumber Salad

  2 servings   10 minutes

INGREDIENTS

- Cucumber: 1 large (approx. 300g), thinly sliced
- Red Onion: 1/4 small (approx. 30g), thinly sliced
- White Vinegar: 2 tablespoons (30ml)
- Olive Oil: 1 tablespoon (15ml)
- Dill: 1 tablespoon, fresh and chopped

Salt and Pepper: To taste

DIRECTIONS

1. **Prepare the Vegetables:**
- Thinly slice the cucumber and red onion. Place them in a mixing bowl.
2. **Make the Dressing:**
- In a small bowl, whisk together the white vinegar, olive oil, salt, and pepper.
3. **Combine the Salad:**
- Pour the dressing over the cucumber and onion slices. Toss gently to coat the vegetables evenly.
- Sprinkle with fresh dill and toss again.
4. **Chill and Serve:**
- Refrigerate the salad for at least 15 minutes to allow the flavors to meld.
- Serve chilled as a refreshing side dish.

Cucumber: Low in calories and hydrating, cucumbers provide a refreshing crunch and are a good source of vitamins K and C.

Red Onion: Adds a sharp, slightly sweet flavor, and is rich in antioxidants.

Dill: Offers a fresh, herbaceous flavor that complements the cucumber and vinegar.

Olive Oil: Contributes healthy fats and adds a smooth texture to the salad.

White Vinegar: Adds acidity, which brightens the flavors and helps to tenderize the cucumber.

Nutritional Information (Per Serving): Calories: ~70 kcal, Total Fat: 7g, Carbohydrates: 4g, Protein: 1g

"Refresh your palate with a crisp cucumber salad—light, crunchy, and a perfect way to celebrate the joy of fresh flavors!"

NOTES _____

Quinoa and Black Bean Salad

  2 servings   🕐 25 minutes

INGREDIENTS

- 1 cup cooked quinoa (approx. 185g)
- 1/2 cup black beans, rinsed and drained (approx. 85g)
- 1/2 cup corn kernels (fresh or canned, approx. 75g)
- 1/2 red bell pepper, diced (approx. 60g)
- 1 tablespoon lime juice (approx. 15ml)

DIRECTIONS

1. **Prepare the Ingredients:**
- Cook quinoa according to package instructions, then let it cool.
- Rinse and drain the black beans.
- Dice the red bell pepper.
2. **Combine the Ingredients:**
- In a large mixing bowl, combine the cooked quinoa, black beans, corn, and diced red bell pepper.
3. **Dress the Salad:**
- Drizzle the lime juice over the salad ingredients.
- Toss the salad gently to ensure even distribution of the lime juice.
4. **Serve:** Serve the Quinoa and Black Bean Salad chilled or at room temperature.

Quinoa: A complete protein, rich in fiber, and provides a nutty flavor and fluffy texture. It's also a good source of iron and magnesium.

Black Beans: Add protein, fiber, and a creamy texture, making the salad more filling and nutritious.

Corn Kernels: Offer sweetness and crunch, along with vitamins A and B, fiber, and antioxidants.

Red Bell Pepper: Adds color, crunch, and a sweet flavor, along with vitamins C and A, and antioxidants.

Lime Juice: Provides a tangy, refreshing flavor and helps brighten the salad, with minimal added calories.

Nutritional Information (Per Serving): Calories: 230 kcal, Total Fat: 4g, Carbohydrates: 40g, Protein: 9g

"Fuel your day with a quinoa and black bean salad—nutritious, hearty, and a tasty reminder that wholesome ingredients can create a delightful dish!"

Serving Suggestions:
- Serve this salad as a light lunch, side dish, or as a topping for grilled chicken or fish.
- It pairs well with a simple avocado dressing or a sprinkle of cilantro for extra flavor.
- Enjoy it with tortilla chips for added crunch.

NOTES _____

Italian Potato Salad

 2 servings 20 minutes

INGREDIENTS

- 2 medium potatoes (approx. 300g)
- 1/4 cup red onion, thinly sliced (approx. 40g)
- 1/4 cup cherry tomatoes, halved (approx. 60g)
- 2 tablespoons olive oil (approx. 30ml)
- 1 tablespoon red wine vinegar (approx. 15ml)

DIRECTIONS

1. **Cook the Potatoes:**
- Wash the potatoes and cut them into bite-sized pieces.
- Place the potatoes in a pot of salted water, bring to a boil, and cook until tender, about 10-12 minutes.
- Drain the potatoes and let them cool slightly.

2. **Prepare the Vegetables:**
- Thinly slice the red onion.
- Halve the cherry tomatoes.

3. **Mix the Salad:**
- In a large mixing bowl, combine the cooked potatoes, sliced red onion, and halved cherry tomatoes.
- Drizzle with olive oil and red wine vinegar.

4. **Toss and Serve:**
- Toss the salad gently to ensure the potatoes are evenly coated with the dressing.
- Serve the Italian Potato Salad at room temperature or chilled.

Potatoes: The main ingredient, providing complex carbohydrates, potassium, and vitamin C. They add a creamy texture when cooked.

Red Onion: Adds a sharp, tangy flavor and a bit of crunch, along with vitamins C and B6, and antioxidants.

Cherry Tomatoes: Provide a sweet and juicy element to the salad, along with vitamins A and C, and lycopene, an antioxidant.

Olive Oil: Offers heart-healthy monounsaturated fats and enhances the flavor of the salad.

Red Wine Vinegar: Adds acidity to balance the flavors and gives the salad a light, refreshing taste.

Nutritional Information (Per Serving): Calories: 260 kcal, Total Fat: 10g, Carbohydrates: 36g, Protein: 4g

"Indulge in the vibrant flavors of Italian potato salad—creamy, herby, and a delicious way to bring a taste of sunshine to your plate!"

Serving Suggestions:
- This Italian Potato Salad pairs well with grilled meats, such as chicken or steak, or as a side dish for barbecues.
- You can add fresh herbs like basil or parsley for extra flavor.
- Serve it alongside crusty Italian bread for a complete meal.

NOTES _____

Sweet Potato Salad

  2 servings · 20 minutes

INGREDIENTS

- 2 medium sweet potatoes (approx. 400g)
- 1/4 cup red onion, thinly sliced (approx. 40g)
- 1/4 cup dried cranberries (approx. 30g)
- 2 tablespoons olive oil (approx. 30ml)
- 1 tablespoon apple cider vinegar (approx. 15ml)

DIRECTIONS

1. **Cook the Sweet Potatoes:**
- Peel and cut the sweet potatoes into bite-sized cubes.
- Place the sweet potatoes in a pot of salted water, bring to a boil, and cook until tender, about 10-12 minutes.
- Drain and allow the sweet potatoes to cool slightly.

2. **Prepare the Ingredients:**
- Thinly slice the red onion.
- Measure out the dried cranberries.

3. **Mix the Salad:**
- In a large mixing bowl, combine the cooked sweet potatoes, sliced red onion, and dried cranberries.
- Drizzle with olive oil and apple cider vinegar.

4. **Toss and Serve:**
- Gently toss the salad to ensure the sweet potatoes are evenly coated with the dressing.
- Serve the Sweet Potato Salad warm or chilled.

Sweet Potatoes: Provide a naturally sweet flavor and are rich in beta-carotene, fiber, and complex carbohydrates.

Red Onion: Adds a bit of sharpness and crunch, along with vitamins C and B6.

Dried Cranberries: Bring a sweet-tart flavor and chewy texture, along with a good source of antioxidants and vitamins.

Olive Oil: Offers healthy fats that enhance the flavors and create a smooth, rich dressing.

Apple Cider Vinegar: Adds acidity to balance the sweetness and gives the salad a refreshing tang.

Nutritional Information (Per Serving): CalorieCalories: 280 kcal, Total Fat: 9g, Carbohydrates: 46g, Protein: 3g

"Enjoy the goodness of sweet potato salad—colorful, hearty, and a delightful reminder to nourish your body with nature's sweet treats!"

Serving Suggestions:

- This Sweet Potato Salad pairs well with roasted meats or grilled chicken.
- Consider adding some fresh herbs like parsley or thyme for additional flavor.
- It can be served as a hearty side dish at holiday meals or barbecues.

NOTES _____

Shrimp and Arugula Salad

 2 servings   15 minutes

INGREDIENTS

- Shrimp: 200g, peeled and deveined
- Arugula (Rucola): 2 cups (approx. 60g)
- Cherry Tomatoes: 1 cup (approx. 150g), halved
- Whole Grain Mustard: 1 tablespoon (approx. 15g)
- Parmesan Cheese: 1/4 cup (approx. 25g), shaved or grated

Optional: lemon Juice, salt and pepper to taste

Olive Oil: 1 tablespoon (approx. 15ml) for cooking shrimps.

DIRECTIONS

1. **Cook the Shrimp:**
- Heat 1 tablespoon of olive oil in a skillet over medium heat.
- Add the shrimp and cook for 2-3 minutes per side, or until pink and opaque.
- Season with salt and pepper to taste. Set aside to cool slightly.
2. **Prepare the Salad:**
- In a large mixing bowl, combine the arugula and cherry tomatoes.
- Add the cooked shrimp to the bowl.
3. **Make the Dressing:**
- In a small bowl, whisk together the whole grain mustard, lemon juice, and a pinch of salt and pepper.
- Drizzle the dressing over the salad and toss gently to combine.
4. **Serve:**
- Divide the salad between two plates.
- Top with shaved Parmesan cheese.
- Serve immediately.

Shrimp: A lean source of protein, low in calories and high in omega-3 fatty acids.

Arugula: Provides vitamins A, C, and K, along with calcium and potassium.

Cherry Tomatoes: Rich in antioxidants, especially lycopene, and add a sweet-tart flavor.

Whole Grain Mustard: Adds tangy flavor with minimal calories and contains whole mustard seeds.

Parmesan Cheese: Adds a salty, savory note and provides calcium and protein.

Nutritional Information (Per Serving): Calories: ~310 kcal, Total Fat: 16g, Carbohydrates: 10g, Protein: 28g

"Treat yourself to a shrimp and arugula salad—light, zesty, and a delicious way to celebrate fresh flavors while keeping your meal vibrant and nutritious!"

NOTES _____

Tuna Salad

 2 servings   10 minutes

INGREDIENTS

- Canned Tuna: 1 can (about 140g drained weight), in water or olive oil, drained
- Mayonnaise: 2 tablespoons (approx. 30g) or olive oil
- Celery: 1/4 cup (approx. 30g), finely chopped
- Red Onion: 2 tablespoons (approx. 20g), finely chopped
- Lemon Juice: 1 tablespoon (approx. 15ml)

Optional Add-ins:

Dijon Mustard: 1 teaspoon (optional, for added tang)

Hard-Boiled Egg: 1, chopped (optional, for extra protein)

Pickles: 1 tablespoon, chopped (optional, for a tangy crunch)

Salt and Pepper To taste

DIRECTIONS

1. **Prepare the Ingredients:**
- Drain the canned tuna and place it in a mixing bowl.
- Finely chop the celery and red onion.

2. **Mix the Salad:**
- Add the mayonnaise, celery, red onion, and lemon juice to the bowl with the tuna. (You may use olive oil if you don't want to use mayonnaise).
- Stir to combine, breaking up the tuna into flakes. Season with salt and pepper to taste.
- Optional: if using, add the Dijon mustard, chopped egg, or pickles and mix well.

3. **Serve:**
- Serve the tuna salad on a bed of lettuce, in a sandwich, or on top of whole grain crackers.
- Garnish with extra celery leaves or herbs if desired.

Tuna: A lean protein source that's also high in omega-3 fatty acids, supporting heart health.

Mayonnaise: Adds creaminess and richness, contributing most of the fat content.

Red Onion: Provides a sharp flavor and is rich in antioxidants.

Celery: Adds a fresh, crunchy texture with minimal calories, along with fibers and vitamins.

Lemon Juice: Brightens the flavors with its acidity, balancing the richness of the mayonnaise.

Nutritional Information (Per Serving): Calories: ~220 kcal (without optional add-ins), Total Fat: 14g, Carbohydrates: 2g, Protein: 20g

"Dig into a classic tuna salad—flaky, flavorful, and a simple way to enjoy a protein-packed meal that nourishes and satisfies!"

Serving Suggestions:
- This tuna salad can be served in various ways: on whole grain bread for a hearty sandwich, with lettuce leaves for a low-carb option, or with crackers for a light snack.
- Pair with a side of fresh fruit or a light vegetable soup to round out the meal.

NOTES _____

- "As you craft your appetizers, think of them as little bites of joy. Each one is a chance to share a piece of your heart—let your creativity flow and enjoy the process of bringing delight to the table."

- "Preparing appetizers is like setting the stage for a wonderful gathering. Let each small dish be a reflection of your warmth and hospitality, filling your kitchen with the anticipation of good times and shared smiles."

- "In every delicate bite you prepare, there's an opportunity to sprinkle a little happiness. As you create your appetizers, let your mind focus on the joy of sharing and the simple pleasures of life's flavorful moments."

Bruschetta

 2 servings   15 minutes

INGREDIENTS

- Baguette Slices: 6 slices (approx. 100g)
- Cherry Tomatoes: 1 cup (approx. 150g), diced
- Fresh Basil: 2 tablespoons, chopped (or fresh parsley)
- Olive Oil: 1 tablespoon (approx. 15ml)
- Garlic: 1 clove, minced

DIRECTIONS

1. **Prepare the Baguette:**
- Preheat your oven to 375°F (190°C).
- Brush both sides of the baguette slices with olive oil.
- Place them on a baking sheet and toast in the oven for 5-7 minutes until golden and crisp.
2. **Prepare the Topping:**
- In a bowl, mix the diced cherry tomatoes, minced garlic, and chopped basil (or parsley).
- Drizzle with olive oil and toss to combine.
3. **Assemble the Bruschetta:**
- Spoon the tomato mixture onto each toasted baguette slice.
4. Serve immediately.

Baguette Slices: Provide carbohydrates and a crunchy base for the toppings.

Cherry Tomatoes: Add freshness and a burst of flavor with a low-calorie count.

Basil: Brings an aromatic and slightly sweet note to the dish.

Olive Oil: Provides healthy fats and enhances the flavor of the tomatoes.

Garlic: Adds a pungent kick that complements the other ingredients.

Nutritional Information (Per Serving): Calories: ~250 kcal, Total Fat: 10g, Carbohydrates: 30g, Protein: 6g

"Enjoy the fresh, vibrant flavors of bruschetta—crispy, colorful, and a delightful reminder to savor every bite of life's simple pleasures!"

Serving Suggestions:
- Serve as an appetizer for an Italian-themed meal or alongside a light salad.
- Pair with a glass of chilled white wine or a sparkling water with lemon.

NOTES _____

Caprese Skewers

 2 servings   10 minutes

INGREDIENTS

- Cherry Tomatoes: 10 (approx. 150g)
- Mozzarella Balls: 10 (approx. 100g)
- Fresh Basil: 10 leaves
- Olive Oil: 1 tablespoon (approx. 15ml)
- Balsamic Glaze: 1 tablespoon (approx. 15ml)

DIRECTIONS

1. **Assemble the Skewers:**
- On each skewer, thread one cherry tomato, one basil leaf, and one mozzarella ball.
2. **Dress the Skewers:**
- Drizzle the skewers with olive oil.
- Finish with a drizzle of balsamic glaze.

Cherry Tomatoes: Offer a sweet and tangy flavor that balances the creaminess of the mozzarella.

Mozzarella Balls: Provide protein and a creamy texture.

Fresh Basil: Adds a fresh, aromatic note.

Olive Oil: Enhances the flavors with its rich, fruity taste.

Balsamic Glaze: Adds a sweet and tangy finish to the skewers.

Nutritional Information (Per Serving): Calories: ~180 kcal, Total Fat: 14g, Carbohydrates: 6g, Protein: 8g

"Elevate your snacking with caprese skewers—bite-sized, colorful, and a delicious way to enjoy fresh flavors on a stick!"

Serving Suggestions:
- Serve as an appetizer at a summer gathering or as a light snack.
- Pair with a crisp white wine or a refreshing iced tea.

NOTES _____

Stuffed Mushrooms

 2 servings   25 minutes

INGREDIENTS

- Button Mushrooms: 8 large (approx. 150g)
- Cream Cheese: 1/4 cup (approx. 60g), softened
- Garlic: 1 clove, minced
- Parmesan Cheese: 2 tablespoons (approx. 20g), grated (or shredded cheese you like)
- Fresh Parsley: 1 tablespoon, chopped

DIRECTIONS

1. **Prepare the Mushrooms:**
- Preheat your oven to 375°F (190°C).
- Remove the stems from the mushrooms and set the caps aside.
2. **Make the Filling:**
- In a bowl, mix the cream cheese, garlic, Parmesan cheese (or shredded cheese), and fresh parsley.
- Spoon the mixture into the mushroom caps.
3. **Bake the Mushrooms:**
- Place the stuffed mushrooms on a baking sheet.
- Bake for 15-20 minutes, or until the mushrooms are tender and the filling is golden.

Button Mushrooms: Low in calories, they provide a meaty texture and a rich, earthy flavor.

Cream Cheese: Adds creaminess and richness to the filling.

Garlic: Infuses the filling with a robust, aromatic flavor.

Parmesan Cheese: Adds a salty, nutty flavor that complements the other ingredients.

Fresh Parsley: Brightens the dish with its fresh, herbaceous notes.

Nutritional Information (Per Serving): Calories: ~150 kcal, Total Fat: 12g, Carbohydrates: 4g, Protein: 6g

"Savor the savory delight of stuffed mushrooms—each bite is a warm, comforting treat that invites you to indulge in good flavors and good company!"

NOTES _____

Hummus and Veggie Platter

  2 servings   10 minutes

INGREDIENTS

- Hummus: 1/2 cup (approx. 120g)
- Carrot Sticks: 1/2 cup (approx. 50g)
- Cucumber Slices: 1/2 cup (approx. 50g)
- Bell Pepper Strips: 1/2 cup (approx. 50g)
- Cherry Tomatoes: 1/2 cup (approx. 75g)

Optional: Sesame Seeds

DIRECTIONS

1. **Prepare the Veggies:**
- Wash (in cool or warm water) and cut the vegetables into sticks, slices, or strips.
- Experiment with different types of vegetables.
2. **Assemble the Platter:**
- Arrange the hummus in the center of a serving platter.
- Surround the hummus with the prepared vegetables.
- Optional: sprinkle the vegetables with sesame seeds.

Hummus: Provides a creamy, protein-rich dip made from chickpeas and tahini.

Carrot: Offer a sweet, crunchy texture and are rich in beta-carotene.

Cucumber: Add a refreshing, hydrating element to the platter.

Bell Pepper: Bring a sweet, crisp flavor and a pop of color.

Cherry Tomatoes: Provide a juicy, tangy contrast to the creamy hummus.

Nutritional Information (Per Serving): Calories: ~200 kcal, Total Fat: 12g, Carbohydrates: 18g, Protein: 5g

"Create a colorful veggie platter with hummus—crunchy, creamy, and a delightful way to celebrate healthy snacking while nourishing your body!"

NOTES _____

Cheese-Stuffed Jalapeños

 2 servings   30 minutes

INGREDIENTS

- Jalapeños: 6 large, halved lengthwise and seeded
- Cream Cheese: 1/2 cup (approx. 115g), softened
- Shredded Cheddar Cheese: 1/2 cup (approx. 50g)
- Bacon Bits or Ham Bits: 2 tablespoons (approx. 14g)
- Chopped Green Onions: 2 tablespoons (approx. 10g)

DIRECTIONS

1. **Prepare the Jalapeños:**
- Preheat your oven to 375°F (190°C).
- Halve the jalapeños lengthwise and remove the seeds and membranes. Be careful when handling jalapeños, as they can irritate your skin and eyes. Latex gloves are highly recommended.
2. **Make the Cheese Filling:** In a mixing bowl, combine the cream cheese, shredded cheddar cheese, bacon or ham bits, and chopped green onions. Mix until well combined.
3. **Stuff the Jalapeños:** Spoon the cheese mixture into each jalapeño half, filling them generously.
4. **Bake the Jalapeños:**
- Place the stuffed jalapeños on a baking sheet lined with parchment paper.
- Bake for 15-20 minutes, or until the jalapeños are tender and the cheese is bubbly and golden.
5. **Serve:** Remove the jalapeños from the oven and let them cool for a few minutes before serving.

Jalapeños: Provide a spicy and crunchy base, adding heat to the dish while being low in calories.

Cream Cheese: Adds a smooth, creamy texture that balances the heat of the jalapeños.

Shredded Cheddar Cheese: Contributes a sharp, rich flavor and creates a melty, gooey texture.

Bacon Bits: Bring a savory, smoky element that complements the cheeses and jalapeños.

Chopped Green Onions: Add a fresh, mild onion flavor, enhancing the overall taste of the filling.

Nutritional Information (Per Serving): Calories: ~250 kcal, Total Fat: 20g, Carbohydrates: 6g, Protein: 10g

"Spice up your snack time with cheese-stuffed jalapeños—crispy, cheesy, and a deliciously bold way to ignite your taste buds!"

Serving Suggestions:

- Serve as an appetizer or snack, perfect for game days, parties, or casual gatherings.
- Pair with a cold beer or a margarita to complement the spiciness.
- These stuffed jalapeños are great on their own or can be served with a dipping sauce like ranch or sour cream to cool down the heat.

NOTES _____

Pigs in a Blanket

 2 servings 25 minutes

INGREDIENTS

- Mini Hot Dogs: 12 pieces (approx. 200g total)
- Crescent Roll Dough: 1 can (approx. 8 oz, or 226g)
- Mustard: 2 tablespoons (approx. 30g)
- Ketchup: 2 tablespoons (approx. 30g)
- Sesame Seeds: 1 tablespoon (approx. 9g)

DIRECTIONS

1. **Preheat your oven** to 375°F (190°C).
2. **Prepare the Dough:** Unroll the crescent roll dough and separate it into triangles. Cut each triangle into smaller strips, depending on the size of your mini hot dogs.
3. **Wrap the Hot Dogs:**
- Spread a small amount of mustard on each strip of dough.
- Place a mini hot dog at the wide end of the dough strip and roll it up towards the pointed end, wrapping the hot dog completely.
- Repeat this process for all 12 hot dogs.
4. **Place the wrapped hot dogs** on a baking sheet lined with parchment paper.
5. **Sprinkle** sesame seeds evenly over the top of each wrapped hot dog.
6. **Bake** in the preheated oven for 12-15 minutes, or until the dough is golden brown and puffed.
7. **Serve** hot with ketchup and extra mustard for dipping.

Mini Hot Dogs: Provide the savory and slightly smoky flavor, as well as protein and fat.

Crescent Roll Dough: Adds a flaky, buttery texture, wrapping the hot dogs in a deliciously soft layer.

Mustard: Adds a tangy, slightly spicy flavor that complements the richness of the dough and hot dogs.

Ketchup: Provides a sweet and tangy contrast, making these snacks more flavorful.

Sesame Seeds: Add a slight nuttiness and extra crunch, enhancing the texture.

Nutritional Information (Per Serving): CalorieCalories: ~280 kcal, Total Fat: 18g, Carbohydrates: 20g, Protein: 9g

"Enjoy the fun of pigs in a blanket—warm, savory, and a playful way to bring comfort and joy to any gathering!"

- Serve as an appetizer, snack, or party food, perfect for casual gatherings or kids' parties.
- Pair with a variety of dipping sauces like honey mustard, BBQ sauce, or ranch dressing.
- These Pigs in a Blanket are great for game days, picnics, or any time you want a quick and tasty treat.

NOTES _____

Mini Pizzas

🍴 2 servings   🕐 20 minutes

INGREDIENTS

- 1/2 can biscuit dough (about 4 biscuits)
- 1/2 cup pizza sauce (approx. 120ml)
- 1/2 cup shredded mozzarella cheese (approx. 60g)
- 6 slices pepperoni (or your favorite topping)
- 1/4 teaspoon dried oregano (for seasoning)

DIRECTIONS

1. **Preheat Oven:** Preheat your oven to 375°F (190°C).
2. **Prepare Dough:** Separate the biscuit dough into individual pieces. Flatten each biscuit slightly with your hands or a rolling pin to form a mini pizza base, about 3-4 inches in diameter.
3. **Add Sauce and Toppings:** Place the flattened biscuit dough on a baking sheet. Spread about 1 tablespoon of pizza sauce on each dough circle. Sprinkle shredded mozzarella cheese evenly over the top, then add a slice or two of pepperoni (or your preferred topping). Sprinkle with a pinch of dried oregano for extra flavor.
4. **Bake:** Bake the mini pizzas in the preheated oven for 10-12 minutes, or until the biscuits are golden and the cheese is melted and bubbly.
5. **Serve:** Let the pizzas cool for a couple of minutes before serving.

Biscuit Dough: Acts as the pizza crust, offering a soft, fluffy texture with a slightly crispy edge.

Pizza Sauce: Adds the classic tomato flavor to the base, with just enough tang and sweetness.

Mozzarella Cheese: Provides the creamy, stretchy cheese element that's essential for a pizza.

Pepperoni: Adds a savory and slightly spicy flavor, complementing the cheese and sauce.

Oregano: A classic pizza herb that adds a touch of warmth and aromatic flavor.

Nutritional Information (Per Serving): CalorieCalories: ~350 kcal, Total Fat: 18g, Carbohydrates: 35g, Protein: 12g

"Have fun with mini pizzas—personal-sized bites of cheesy, saucy goodness that are perfect for sharing or enjoying all to yourself!"

NOTES _____

Garlic Parmesan Pretzels

  2 servings   15 minutes

INGREDIENTS

- Pretzel Rods: 8 pieces (approx. 80g)
- Parmesan Cheese: 1/4 cup, grated (approx. 25g)
- Garlic Powder: 1/2 teaspoon (approx. 2g)
- Butter: 1 tablespoon, melted (approx. 15g)
- Fresh Parsley: 1 tablespoon, chopped (approx. 3g)

DIRECTIONS

1. **Preheat your oven** to 350°F (175°C).
2. **Prepare the Pretzels:**
- Place the pretzel rods on a baking sheet lined with parchment paper.
- In a small bowl, mix the melted butter with garlic powder.
3. **Coat the Pretzels:**
- Brush the pretzel rods with the garlic butter mixture.
- Sprinkle the grated Parmesan cheese evenly over the pretzels.
4. **Bake** in the preheated oven for 5-7 minutes, or until the cheese is melted and slightly golden.
5. **Add Fresh Parsley:**
- Remove from the oven and immediately sprinkle with chopped parsley.
6. **Serve:** Allow the pretzels to cool slightly before serving.

Pretzel Rods: Provide a crunchy texture and a salty flavor, serving as the base for the snack.

Parmesan Cheese: Adds a rich, nutty flavor and a slightly crispy texture when baked.

Garlic Powder: Infuses the pretzels with a savory garlic flavor, enhancing the overall taste.

Butter: Helps the Parmesan cheese stick to the pretzels and adds a rich, buttery flavor.

Fresh Parsley: Adds a touch of freshness and color, balancing the richness of the cheese and butter.

Nutritional Information (Per Serving): Calories: ~200 kcal, Total Fat: 10g, Carbohydrates: 22g, Protein: 6g

"Savor the irresistible flavor of garlic parmesan pretzels—crispy, cheesy, and a deliciously warm treat that makes every snack time special!"

Serving Suggestions:
- Serve as a snack or appetizer at parties, game days, or casual gatherings.
- Pair with dips like marinara sauce, ranch dressing, or mustard for added flavor.
- These Garlic Parmesan Pretzels are perfect for munching on their own or alongside a cheese board or charcuterie platter.

NOTES _____

Deviled Eggs

🍴 2 servings   🕐 25 minutes

INGREDIENTS

- Eggs: 2 large eggs
- Mayonnaise: 1 tablespoon (approx. 15g)
- Whole Grain Mustard: 1/2 teaspoon (approx. 2.5g)
- Paprika: A pinch, for garnish
- Chives: 1/2 teaspoon, chopped (approx. 1g)

DIRECTIONS

1. **Boil the Eggs:**
- Place the eggs in a saucepan and cover them with water. Bring to a boil over medium heat.
- Once boiling, remove from heat and cover the pan. Let the eggs sit for 10-12 minutes.
2. **Cool and Peel:**
- Drain the hot water and transfer the eggs to an ice bath to cool for 5 minutes.
- Peel the eggs and cut them in half lengthwise.
3. **Prepare the Filling:**
- Remove the yolks and place them in a small bowl.
- Mash the yolks with a fork, then mix in the mayonnaise and whole grain mustard until smooth.
4. **Fill the Eggs:**
- Spoon or pipe the yolk mixture back into the egg whites.
- Garnish with a sprinkle of paprika and chopped chives.
5. **Serve:** Arrange on a platter and serve chilled.

Eggs: Provide high-quality protein, healthy fats, and essential nutrients like choline and vitamin D.

Mayonnaise: Adds creaminess and richness to the filling, contributing to the overall flavor.

Whole Grain Mustard: Offers a tangy and slightly spicy flavor that enhances the taste of the deviled eggs.

Paprika: Adds a mild, smoky flavor and a pop of color to the dish.

Chives: Provide a fresh, onion-like flavor that complements the creamy filling.

Nutritional Information (Per Serving): Calories: ~130 kcal, Total Fat: 11g, Carbohydrates: 1g, Protein: 6g

"Delight in the classic charm of deviled eggs—creamy, tangy, and a perfect little bite of happiness for any occasion!"

Serving Suggestions:
- Serve as a classic appetizer at brunches, picnics, or holiday gatherings.
- Pair with fresh vegetables, salads, or other finger foods.
- These Deviled Eggs can be customized with additional toppings like bacon bits, pickles, or hot sauce for extra flavor.

NOTES _____

Cucumber and Shrimp Appetizer

 2 servings 15 minutes

INGREDIENTS

- Cucumber: 1 large, sliced into rounds
- Cooked Shrimp: 12 medium-sized shrimp, peeled and deveined
- Cream Cheese: 2 tablespoons, softened
- Fresh Dill: 1 tablespoon, chopped
- Lemon Zest: 1 teaspoon

DIRECTIONS

1. **Prepare the Cucumber:**
- Slice the cucumber into 12 rounds, each about 1/4 inch thick.
2. **Prepare the Shrimp:**
- Ensure the shrimp are cooked, peeled, and deveined. If using fresh shrimp, boil them in salted water until pink and opaque, about 2-3 minutes.
3. **Assemble the Appetizers:**
- Spread a small dollop of cream cheese onto each cucumber slice.
- Place one shrimp on top of the cream cheese.
- Sprinkle the shrimp with fresh dill and lemon zest.
4. **Chill and Serve:**
- Arrange the appetizers on a serving platter and refrigerate for 10-15 minutes before serving to keep them cool.

Cucumber: Provides a refreshing and crunchy base with minimal calories, rich in hydration and fiber.

Cooked Shrimp: A lean source of protein, low in calories, and adds a delicate seafood flavor.

Cream Cheese: Adds creaminess and a slight tang, balancing the fresh flavors with richness.

Fresh Dill: Enhances the dish with a fragrant herb flavor, complementing the shrimp.

Lemon Zest: Adds a bright citrus note that cuts through the creaminess and enhances the shrimp's natural flavor.

Nutritional Information (Per Serving): Calories: ~120 kcal, Total Fat: 6g, Carbohydrates: 4g, Protein: 12g

"Indulge in a refreshing cucumber and shrimp appetizer—light, zesty, and a delightful way to elevate your taste buds with a burst of flavor!"

Serving Suggestions:
- Serve these appetizers chilled for a refreshing and light starter.
- Pair with a crisp white wine, such as a Sauvignon Blanc, or a sparkling water with lemon.
- These appetizers are perfect for summer gatherings, cocktail parties, or as a light bite before a main course.

NOTES _____

Cheese, Fruits, and Nuts Platter

 2 servings 15 minutes

INGREDIENTS

- Cheese: 3 types (approx. 150g total), such as Brie, Cheddar, and Gouda
- Fresh Fruits: 1 cup mixed, such as grapes, apple slices, and figs
- Nuts: 1/4 cup mixed, such as almonds, walnuts, and pecans
- Crackers or Breadsticks: 6-8 pieces
- Honey or Jam: 2 tablespoons for drizzling or dipping

DIRECTIONS

1. **Prepare the Cheese:**
- Slice or cube the cheese varieties, arranging them on a platter.
- Allow the cheese to come to room temperature before serving to enhance flavor.
2. **Add the Fruits:**
- Wash and slice the fruits. Arrange them around the cheese on the platter.
3. **Add the Nuts:**
- Scatter the mixed nuts around the cheese and fruit.
4. **Add the Crackers/Breadsticks:**
- Place the crackers or breadsticks on the side of the platter.
5. **Drizzle with Honey or Add Jam:**
- Drizzle the honey over the cheese or fruits, or serve the jam in a small bowl for dipping.

Cheese: Provides a rich source of protein, calcium, and fats, offering a variety of textures and flavors.

Fresh Fruits: Add sweetness, freshness, and a range of vitamins and antioxidants.

Nuts: Offer a crunchy texture and are rich in healthy fats, protein, and fiber.

Crackers/Breadsticks: Provide a crunchy contrast to the soft cheeses and fruits.

Honey/Jam: Adds a touch of sweetness that pairs beautifully with the salty and savory flavors of the cheese.

Nutritional Information (Per Serving): Calories: ~450 kcal, Total Fat: 30g, Carbohydrates: 25g, Protein: 18g

"Create a beautiful cheese, fruits, and nuts platter—each bite is a harmonious blend of flavors and textures, perfect for sharing joy and celebration!"

Serving Suggestions:
- SerServe as an appetizer or a light snack, ideal for sharing.
- Pair with a glass of wine, such as a white Sauvignon Blanc or a red Pinot Noir, or a refreshing sparkling water.

NOTES _____

- "As you prepare dinner, let each movement be mindful and gentle. The evening is a time for reflection and rest—let the meal you create be a symbol of gratitude for the day and a nourishing way to end it."

- "In the quiet moments of preparing dinner, find peace in the rhythm of chopping, stirring, and seasoning. This is your time to unwind and pour love into every dish, creating a meal that brings joy to you and those around you."

- "Cooking dinner is a beautiful way to close the day —each ingredient a reminder of the abundance in your life. As you prepare the meal, let gratitude fill your heart, knowing that the time and care you put into it will bring warmth and happiness."

One-Pan Lemon Garlic Chicken

 2 servings   30 minutes

INGREDIENTS

- Chicken Thighs: 4 pieces (approx. 400g)
- Lemon: 1, sliced
- Garlic: 4 cloves, minced
- Olive Oil: 2 tablespoons (approx. 30ml)
- Fresh Thyme: 2 sprigs

Optional: Salt and Pepper To taste

DIRECTIONS

1. **Preheat the Oven:**
- Preheat your oven to 375°F (190°C).
2. **Season the Chicken:**
- Rub the chicken thighs with olive oil, minced garlic, and season with salt, pepper, and thyme.
3. **Sear the Chicken:**
- Heat a skillet over medium-high heat and sear the chicken thighs skin-side down until golden brown.
4. **Add Lemon and Roast:**
- Add lemon slices and transfer the skillet to the oven. Roast for 20-25 minutes or until the chicken is cooked through.
5. **Serve:**
- Garnish with extra lemon slices and thyme.

Chicken Thighs: Provide juicy, flavorful protein.

Lemon: Adds bright, tangy flavor.

Garlic: Infuses the dish with a rich, savory aroma.

Olive Oil: Adds healthy fats and helps crisp up the chicken.

Thyme: Offers earthy, herbal notes.

Nutritional Information (Per Serving): Calories: ~400 kcal, Total Fat: 25g, Carbohydrates: 5g, Protein: 35g

"Cook up a burst of flavor with one-pan lemon garlic chicken—where juicy chicken meets the bright zing of lemon, making mealtime a breeze!"

Serving Suggestions:
- Serve with roasted vegetables or a light salad for a balanced meal.

NOTES _____

Chicken and Rice Skillet

 2 servings   25 minutes

INGREDIENTS

- 2 chicken thighs (boneless and skinless, approx. 200g)
- 1/2 cup rice (uncooked, approx. 90g)
- 1/2 bell pepper (chopped, approx. 50g)
- 1/4 onion (chopped, approx. 30g)
- 1 cup chicken broth (approx. 240ml)

DIRECTIONS

1. **Season Chicken:** Season the chicken thighs with salt and pepper on both sides.
2. **Brown the Chicken:** Heat a skillet over medium heat and add a small amount of oil. Brown the chicken thighs for about 3-4 minutes on each side until they are golden. Remove the chicken and set it aside.
3. **Sauté Vegetables:** In the same skillet, add the chopped onion and bell pepper. Sauté for about 3-4 minutes until softened and fragrant.
4. **Add Rice and Broth:** Stir the rice into the skillet with the vegetables, ensuring it's well mixed. Pour in the chicken broth and bring the mixture to a simmer.
5. **Cook the Chicken and Rice:** Return the browned chicken thighs to the skillet, nestling them on top of the rice. Cover the skillet with a lid and reduce the heat to low. Cook for 18-20 minutes, or until the rice is tender and the chicken is fully cooked through (internal temperature of 165°F/74°C).
6. **Serve:** Once the rice is cooked and the chicken is done, remove from heat. Let it rest for a few minutes before serving.

Chicken Thighs: A juicy and flavorful protein source that pairs well with the rice and vegetables.

Rice: Provides the base of the dish, soaking up the flavors of the broth and vegetables.

Bell Pepper: Adds a slight sweetness and a crunchy texture, balancing the savory chicken.

Onion: Adds depth and flavor to the dish when sautéed.

Chicken Broth: Provides liquid to cook the rice and infuses the dish with rich, savory flavor.

Nutritional Information (Per Serving): Calories: ~400 kcal, Total Fat: 12g, Carbohydrates: 45g, Protein: 25g

"Cook up comfort with a chicken and rice skillet—a hearty, one-pan dish that's full of flavor and brings warmth to your table with ease!"

Serving Suggestions:

- Garnish with Fresh Herbs: Add a sprinkle of fresh parsley or cilantro for added color and flavor.
- Vegetable Sides: Serve with a side of steamed vegetables, like broccoli or green beans, for a more complete meal.
- Lemon Wedges: A squeeze of fresh lemon over the dish can brighten the flavors and add a tangy contrast to the savory components.

NOTES _____

Beef Stroganoff

🍴 2 servings   🕐 20 minutes

INGREDIENTS

- Beef Strips: 200g
- Mushrooms: 1 cup, sliced (approx. 80g)
- Sour Cream: 1/4 cup (approx. 60ml)
- Onion: 1/4 cup, chopped (approx. 40g)
- Beef Broth (or Water): 1 cup (approx. 240ml)

DIRECTIONS

1. **Sauté the Onion and Beef:**
- Heat oil in a pan and sauté onions until softened, then add beef strips and cook until browned.
2. **Add Mushrooms and Broth:**
- Stir in mushrooms and beef broth, simmering for 10 minutes.
3. **Finish with Sour Cream:**
- Stir in the sour cream and cook for another 2 minutes until smooth.
4. **Serve:**
- Serve over egg noodles or rice.

Beef Strips: Provide rich protein and flavor.

Mushrooms: Add umami and texture.

Sour Cream: Creates creaminess with tang.

Onion: Adds sweetness and depth.

Beef Broth: Enhances savory flavors.

Nutritional Information (Per Serving): Calories: ~450 kcal, Total Fat: 25g, Carbohydrates: 10g, Protein: 35g

"Treat yourself to the hearty warmth of beef stroganoff—an inviting blend of savory beef and creamy sauce that turns any dinner into a cozy celebration!"

Serving Suggestions:
- Serve with egg noodles or mashed potatoes.

NOTES _____

Pork Chops with Apple Sauce

 2 servings 15 minutes

INGREDIENTS

- Pork Chops: 2 (approx. 300g)
- Apple: 1, peeled and sliced
- Apple Sauce: 1/4 cup (approx. 60ml)
- Olive Oil: 1 tablespoon (approx. 15ml)
- Cinnamon: 1/4 teaspoon

DIRECTIONS

1. **Season the Pork Chops:**
- Season the pork chops with salt, pepper, and a pinch of cinnamon.
2. **Cook the Pork Chops:**
- Heat olive oil in a skillet over medium-high heat. Sear the pork chops for 4-5 minutes on each side until browned and cooked through.
3. **Prepare the Apple Sauce:**
- In the same skillet, add apple slices and sauté until softened (about 3-4 minutes). Stir in the apple sauce and remaining cinnamon, and cook for another minute.
4. **Serve:**
- Top the pork chops with the apple sauce and serve.

Pork Chops: Provide rich protein and savory flavor.

Apple: Adds sweetness and texture to balance the savory pork.

Apple Sauce: Enhances the sweetness and ties the dish together.

Olive Oil: Adds healthy fats and aids in cooking.

Cinnamon: Adds warmth and enhances the apple's sweetness.

Nutritional Information (Per Serving): Calories: ~350 kcal, Total Fat: 20g, Carbohydrates: 15g, Protein: 28g

"Savor the delicious contrast of pork chops with apple sauce—juicy, tender, and a delightful blend of savory and sweet that brings comfort to your plate!"

Serving Suggestions:
- Serve with roasted vegetables or mashed potatoes for a comforting meal.

NOTES _____

Lamb Chops with Rosemary

 2 servings 45 minutes

INGREDIENTS

- 4 lamb chops (approx. 300g total)
- 2 tablespoons olive oil (approx. 30ml)
- 2 cloves garlic, minced
- 1 teaspoon fresh rosemary, chopped (or 1/2 teaspoon dried rosemary)
- Salt and Pepper to taste

DIRECTIONS

1. **Marinate the Lamb Chops:** In a small bowl, combine the minced garlic, chopped rosemary, olive oil, salt, and pepper. Rub this mixture evenly over the lamb chops. Let the lamb chops marinate for at least 30 minutes, or refrigerate them overnight for more intense flavor.
2. **Heat the Pan:** Heat a large skillet or grill pan over medium-high heat. Once the pan is hot, add a tablespoon of olive oil if using a skillet.
3. **Cook the Lamb Chops:** Place the lamb chops in the hot skillet or on the grill. Sear for about 3-4 minutes on each side for medium-rare, or 5-6 minutes per side for medium to well-done, depending on the thickness of the chops.
4. **Rest the Meat:** Once cooked to your preferred doneness, remove the lamb chops from the pan and let them rest for about 5 minutes to allow the juices to redistribute.
5. **Serve:** Serve the lamb chops with your choice of side dishes, such as roasted vegetables, mashed potatoes, or a simple green salad.

Lamb Chops: Rich in protein and healthy fats, lamb chops offer a tender and flavorful cut of meat. The fat content contributes to its juicy texture.

Garlic: Adds a robust flavor that complements the richness of the lamb.

Rosemary: A classic herb pairing with lamb, rosemary enhances the flavor with earthy, piney notes.

Olive Oil: Helps to sear the meat and adds a healthy fat component.

Salt and Pepper: Essential seasonings that bring out the natural flavors of the lamb.

Nutritional Information (Per Serving): Calories: ~350 kcal, Total Fat: 25g, Carbohydrates: 1g, Protein: 28g

"Savor the rich flavor of lamb chops with rosemary—perfectly tender, aromatic, and a classic dish that brings an herbaceous touch to every bite!"

NOTES _____

Turkey Meatballs

🍴 2 servings   🕐 25 minutes

INGREDIENTS

- Ground Turkey: 250g
- Breadcrumbs: 1/4 cup (approx. 30g)
- Parmesan Cheese: 2 tablespoons (approx. 10g), grated
- Egg: 1 large
- Garlic: 2 cloves, minced

Optional: Fresh Parsley: 2 tablespoons, chopped, Salt: 1/2 teaspoon, Black Pepper: 1/4 teaspoon, Olive Oil: 1 tablespoon (for cooking)

DIRECTIONS

1. **Prepare the Mixture:**
- In a large mixing bowl, combine ground turkey, breadcrumbs, Parmesan cheese, egg, minced garlic. Optional: add parsley, salt, and black pepper. Mix until well combined.
2. **Form the Meatballs:**
- Roll the mixture into small meatballs, about 1-1.5 inches in diameter. You should get about 10 meatballs.
3. **Cook the Meatballs:**
- Heat olive oil in a large skillet over medium heat. Add the meatballs, cooking for 5-6 minutes on each side, until browned and cooked through (internal temperature should reach 165°F/75°C).
4. **Serve:**
- Serve the turkey meatballs hot, garnished with additional parsley. Pair with a marinara sauce, or serve over pasta, in a sandwich, or alongside vegetables.

Ground Turkey: A lean source of protein, lower in fat compared to beef or pork.

Breadcrumbs: Help bind the mixture and add texture.

Parmesan Cheese: Adds a salty, umami flavor to enhance the taste of the meatballs.

Egg: Binds the ingredients together to form a cohesive meatball.

Garlic: Add depth and freshness to the flavor profile.

Nutritional Information (Per Serving): Calories: ~300 kcal, Total Fat: 15g, Carbohydrates: 8g, Protein: 30g

"Relish the light and tasty bite of turkey meatballs—crafted with care, they bring a healthy twist to comfort food, making every meal feel like a treat!"

NOTES _____

Easy Spaghetti Carbonara

 2 servings 15 minutes

INGREDIENTS

- Spaghetti: 160g
- Bacon: 4 slices, chopped (approx. 80g)
- Eggs: 2 large
- Parmesan Cheese: 1/4 cup, grated (approx. 25g)
- Black Pepper: To taste

DIRECTIONS

1. **Cook Spaghetti:**
- Cook pasta according to package instructions.
2. **Cook Bacon:**
- In a skillet, cook bacon until crispy.
3. **Mix Eggs and Cheese:**
- Whisk eggs and Parmesan together in a bowl.
4. **Combine:**
- Toss cooked pasta with bacon and remove from heat. Quickly stir in egg mixture and black pepper.
5. **Serve:**
- Serve immediately with extra Parmesan.

Spaghetti: Provides carbs and energy.

Bacon: Adds savory crunch and fat

Eggs: Make the sauce creamy and rich.

Parmesan Cheese: Adds sharp, nutty flavor and provides a source of calcium.

Black Pepper: Enhances the dish with spice.

Nutritional Information (Per Serving): Calories: ~500 kcal, Total Fat: 25g, Carbohydrates: 45g, Protein: 25g

"Delight in the simplicity of easy spaghetti carbonara—creamy, savory, and a quick dish that transforms everyday ingredients into a comforting masterpiece!"

Serving Suggestions:
- Serve with garlic bread or a side salad.

NOTES _____

Creamy Tomato Pasta

  2 servings   20 minutes

INGREDIENTS

- Pasta: 200g (spaghetti, penne, or your choice)
- Tomato Sauce: 1 cup (approx. 240ml)
- Heavy Cream: 1/2 cup (approx. 120ml)
- Garlic: 2 cloves, minced
- Parmesan Cheese: 1/4 cup (approx. 25g), grated

Optional; Olive Oil: 1 tablespoon, Fresh Basil: 2 tablespoons, chopped, Salt and Pepper to taste

DIRECTIONS

1. **Cook the Pasta:** Bring a large pot of salted water to a boil and cook the pasta according to package instructions. Drain and set aside.
2. **Sauté the Garlic:** In a large skillet, heat olive oil over medium heat. Add minced garlic and sauté for 1-2 minutes until fragrant.
3. **Add Tomato Sauce:** Pour in the tomato sauce, stirring to combine with the garlic. Let it simmer for 5 minutes.
4. **Stir in Cream:** Reduce heat to low, and slowly stir in the heavy cream. Cook for another 3-4 minutes until the sauce is creamy and heated through.
5. **Toss the Pasta:** Add the cooked pasta to the skillet, tossing it in the sauce until fully coated.
6. **Add Cheese and Season:** Stir in grated Parmesan cheese and season with salt and pepper to taste.
7. **Serve:** Serve hot. Optional: garnish with fresh basil and extra Parmesan cheese.

Pasta: Provides carbohydrates and acts as the base of the dish.

Tomato Sauce: Brings acidity and sweetness to balance the creaminess.

Heavy Cream: Adds richness and creaminess to the sauce.

Garlic: Enhances the savory depth of flavor.

Parmesan Cheese: Adds saltiness and umami, balancing the richness of the cream.

Nutritional Information (Per Serving): Calories: ~500 kcal, Total Fat: 25g, Carbohydrates: 55g, Protein: 15g

"Twirl your fork in creamy tomato pasta—rich, comforting, and a delightful fusion of flavors that turns a simple meal into a satisfying indulgence!"

Serving Suggestions:
- Pair with a green side salad and garlic bread for a complete meal.

NOTES _____

Baked Salmon with Dill

 2 servings   15 minutes

INGREDIENTS

- Salmon Fillets: 2 (approx. 200g each)
- Lemon: 1, sliced
- Dill: 2 tablespoons, chopped
- Olive Oil: 1 tablespoon (approx. 15ml)
- Garlic: 2 cloves, minced

DIRECTIONS

1. **Preheat the Oven:**
- Preheat to 400°F (200°C).
2. **Season the Salmon:**
- Place salmon on a baking sheet. Drizzle with olive oil, garlic, dill, and lemon slices.
3. **Bake:**
- Bake for 12-15 minutes until the salmon is flaky.
4. **Serve:**
- Garnish with extra dill and lemon.

Salmon: Rich in omega-3 fatty

Lemon: Adds brightness and acidity.

Dill: Brings fresh, herby flavors.

Olive Oil: Provides healthy monounsaturated fats. Adds richness.

Garlic: Adds depth and savoriness and has anti-inflammatory properties.

Nutritional Information (Per Serving): Calories: ~350 kcal, Total Fat: 22g, Carbohydrates: 4g, Protein: 30g

"Experience the vibrant flavors of baked salmon with dill—tender, fragrant, and a simple way to bring a taste of the sea to your table!"

Serving Suggestions:
- Pair with roasted asparagus or a side salad.

NOTES _____

Turmeric-Spiced Grilled Mackerel

  2 servings   40 minutes

INGREDIENTS

- 2 mackerel fillets (about 200g each)
- 1 teaspoon turmeric powder (approx. 2g)
- 2 tablespoons olive oil (approx. 30ml)
- 2 cloves garlic, minced (approx. 6g)
- 1/4 teaspoon black pepper (approx. 1g)

DIRECTIONS

1. **Prepare the marinade:** In a small bowl, combine turmeric, minced garlic, olive oil, and black pepper.
2. **Marinate the mackerel:** Rub the marinade evenly over the mackerel fillets. Let them sit for 15-20 minutes to absorb the flavors.
3. **Preheat the grill:** Heat your grill or grill pan to medium-high heat.
4. **Grill the mackerel:** Place the marinated fillets on the grill, skin-side down. Grill for about 4-5 minutes per side, or until the fish is cooked through and flakes easily with a fork.
5. **Serve:** Plate the grilled mackerel fillets with a side of fresh vegetables, rice, or salad.

Mackerel Fillets: A rich source of omega-3 fatty acids, which are beneficial for heart health. Mackerel is also high in protein and provides essential vitamins and minerals.

Turmeric: Adds a warm, earthy flavor and has powerful anti-inflammatory and antioxidant properties due to the active compound, curcumin.

Olive Oil: A healthy fat that enhances the absorption of curcumin from turmeric. Olive oil is rich in monounsaturated fats and antioxidants.

Garlic: Contributes a bold, savory flavor while providing antimicrobial and anti-inflammatory benefits.

Black Pepper: Not only enhances the flavor but also helps increase the absorption of curcumin from the turmeric, making the dish even more health-beneficial.

Nutritional Information (Per Serving): Calories: ~300 kcal, Total Fat: 22g, Carbohydrates: 2g, Protein: 25g

"Elevate your dining experience with turmeric-spiced grilled mackerel—flaky, flavorful, and a vibrant dish that adds a burst of color and health to your table!"

Serving Suggestions:
- Serve this turmeric-spiced grilled mackerel with a light side salad of mixed greens or a simple quinoa salad.
- You can also accompany it with roasted vegetables or a squeeze of lemon juice for added freshness.

NOTES _____

Garlic Butter Shrimp

 2 servings   10 minutes

INGREDIENTS

- Large Shrimp: 12, peeled and deveined (approx. 200g)
- Butter: 3 tablespoons (approx. 45g)
- Garlic: 3 cloves, minced
- Lemon Juice: 1 tablespoon (approx. 15ml)
- Fresh Parsley: 2 tablespoons, chopped

DIRECTIONS

1. **Prepare the Shrimp:**
- Rinse and pat dry the shrimp.
2. **Melt the Butter:**
- In a skillet over medium heat, melt the butter.
3. **Cook the Garlic:**
- Add minced garlic and sauté for 1 minute until fragrant.
4. **Cook the Shrimp:**
- Add the shrimp to the pan and cook for 2-3 minutes on each side until pink and opaque.
5. **Add Lemon and Parsley:**
- Drizzle with lemon juice and sprinkle with fresh parsley. Stir to coat the shrimp in the garlic butter.
6. **Serve:**
- Serve hot with a side of crusty bread or over pasta.

Shrimp: Provides lean protein and omega-3 fatty acids.

Butter: Adds richness and a creamy texture.

Garlic: Infuses the dish with a savory, aromatic flavor.

Lemon Juice: Adds a bright, tangy balance to the richness of the butter.

Parsley: Freshens up the dish with herbaceous notes.

Nutritional Information (Per Serving): Calories: ~260 kcal, Total Fat: 20g, Carbohydrates: 2g, Protein: 18g

"Indulge in the rich flavors of garlic butter shrimp—succulent, savory, and a simple dish that makes every bite feel like a gourmet experience!"

Serving Suggestions:
- Serve with rice, pasta, or alongside a fresh green salad.

NOTES _____

Seafood Paella

2 servings   40 minutes

INGREDIENTS

- 1 cup rice (approx. 200g)
- 2 cups chicken broth (approx. 500ml)
- 1/2 teaspoon saffron (or a pinch, about 0.25g)
- 1 red bell pepper, diced (approx. 100g)
- 8 medium shrimp, peeled and deveined (approx. 120g) (or seafood cocktail)

Optional: Green Beans, Salt and pepper to taste, Olive Oil for cooking, Lemon wedges for serving

DIRECTIONS

1. **Prepare the Shrimp:** If using raw shrimp, peel and devein them, and set them aside. You'll add them during the final 5 minutes of cooking to ensure they don't overcook.
2. **Toast the Rice and Saffron:** Heat 1 tablespoon of olive oil in a large pan over medium heat. Add the diced bell pepper and sauté until softened, about 5 minutes. Stir in the rice and saffron, cooking for about 2 minutes, until the rice starts to become slightly translucent and the saffron releases its fragrance and color.
3. **Add the Broth:** Slowly pour in the chicken broth and bring the mixture to a boil. Once it starts boiling, reduce the heat to a low simmer. Stir occasionally to ensure the rice cooks evenly and absorbs the broth. Season with a pinch of salt and pepper.
4. **Simmer Until Done:** Let the rice simmer for about 15-20 minutes, or until most of the liquid is absorbed and the rice is nearly cooked through. If needed, you can add a little extra broth or water if the pan dries out before the rice is tender.
5. **Cook the Shrimp:** In the last 5 minutes of cooking, gently place the shrimp on top of the rice. Cover the pan and allow the shrimp to cook through, turning pink and opaque, about 5 minutes.
6. **Final Touches:** Remove the pan from heat once the shrimp is cooked and the rice has absorbed the broth. Let the paella rest for a few minutes before serving to let the flavors meld.

Rice: The starch base of the dish, providing a filling component rich in carbohydrates.

Saffron: An essential spice that gives the paella its distinct golden color and subtle, earthy flavor.

Shrimp: A protein source that also contributes a mild sweetness and firm texture to the dish.

Bell Pepper: Adds a vibrant, sweet crunch and balances the richness of the rice and shrimp.

Chicken Broth: Adds depth and flavor, ensuring the rice absorbs the right amount of liquid while cooking.

Nutritional Information (Per Serving): Calories: ~450 kcal, Total Fat: 6g, Carbohydrates: 80g, Protein: 25g

"Transport yourself to the coast with seafood paella—each bite a savory blend of tender seafood, saffron, and rice, capturing the vibrant essence of the sea!"

Serving Suggestions:
- Serve the paella with lemon wedges on the side to brighten the flavors.
- Pair with a fresh green salad, such as arugula or mixed greens, dressed in a light vinaigrette.
- For a more authentic Spanish-style paella, feel free to add other seafood like mussels, clams, or squid, or even some chorizo for an extra layer of flavor.

NOTES _____

Vegetable Stir-Fry

 2 servings   15 minutes

INGREDIENTS

- Mixed Vegetables (bell peppers, broccoli, snap peas): 2 cups (200g)
- Soy Sauce: 2 tablespoons (30ml)
- Ginger: 1 teaspoon, minced
- Garlic: 2 cloves, minced
- Olive Oil: 1 tablespoon (15ml)

Optional: 1 tablespoon sesame seeds for garnish

DIRECTIONS

1. **Prepare the Vegetables:**
- Bell Peppers: Cut into thin strips.
- Broccoli: Cut into small florets.
- Snap Peas: Trim the ends if needed.
- Experiment with different types of vegetables.
2. **StirCook the Vegetables:**
- Heat olive oil in a large skillet or wok over medium-high heat.
- Add minced garlic and ginger, stir for about 30 seconds until fragrant.
- Add the mixed vegetables to the skillet. Stir-fry for 5-7 minutes, until the vegetables are tender but still crisp.
3. **Add Sauce:**
- Pour the soy sauce over the vegetables and stir well to coat.
- Stir-fry for another 1-2 minutes to allow the sauce to heat through and flavors to combine.
4. **Serve:** Remove from heat, sprinkle with sesame seeds if desired, and serve hot.

Mixed Vegetables: Provide essential vitamins, fiber, and antioxidants. Each vegetable contributes unique nutrients.

Soy Sauce: Adds umami and a savory depth to the stir-fry.

Olive Oil: A healthy fat source that helps cook the vegetables while adding flavor.

Ginger: Ginger adds a spicy, warm flavor to the dish. It has anti-inflammatory properties, antioxidants and can boost the immune system.

Garlic: Garlic provides a savory, aromatic foundation to the stir-fry. It has immune-boosting properties, anti-inflammatory and antimicrobial.

Nutritional Information (Per Serving): Calories: ~150 kcal, Total Fat: 7g, Carbohydrates: 15g, Protein: 4g

"Whip up a vibrant vegetable stir-fry—colorful, crisp, and a quick way to savor the crunch of fresh veggies in a burst of flavor!"

NOTES _____

Broccoli with Cheese

 2 servings 15 minutes

INGREDIENTS

- 2 cups broccoli florets (approx. 200g)
- 1/2 cup shredded cheddar cheese (approx. 60g)
- 1 tablespoon butter (approx. 15g)
- 1 tablespoon flour (approx. 8g)
- 1/2 cup milk (approx. 120ml)

DIRECTIONS

1. **Cook the Broccoli:** Steam or boil the broccoli florets for 4-5 minutes until they are tender but still crisp. Drain and set aside.
2. **Prepare the Cheese Sauce:** In a small saucepan, melt the butter over medium heat. Once melted, whisk in the flour to create a roux. Cook for 1-2 minutes, stirring constantly, until the mixture is lightly golden.
3. **Add the Milk:** Gradually whisk in the milk, ensuring no lumps form. Continue stirring and cook for 3-4 minutes, or until the mixture begins to thicken.
4. **Melt the Cheese:** Remove the saucepan from heat and stir in the shredded cheddar cheese until smooth and melted. If the sauce is too thick, add a little more milk to reach the desired consistency.
5. **Combine and Serve:** Pour the cheese sauce over the cooked broccoli and gently toss to coat the florets evenly. Serve warm.

Broccoli: Rich in fiber, vitamins, and minerals, broccoli is a healthy base for this dish. It adds texture and nutrition.

Cheddar Cheese: Provides a creamy, savory flavor, with fats and protein to enrich the broccoli.

Butter: Adds richness and forms the base of the roux for the cheese sauce.

Flour: Helps thicken the sauce, giving it a smooth, velvety texture.

Milk: Adds creaminess to the cheese sauce and helps create the smooth consistency of the dish.

Nutritional Information (Per Serving): Calories: ~230 kcal, Total Fat: 16g, Carbohydrates: 10g, Protein: 10g

"Brighten your plate with broccoli and cheese—crisp, tender florets smothered in creamy, melty cheese for a comforting and nutritious bite!"

Serving Suggestions:
- Main Course Side: This dish pairs well with roasted chicken, steak, or grilled fish as a cheesy, vegetable side.
- Top with Breadcrumbs: For added crunch, sprinkle toasted breadcrumbs on top of the broccoli before serving.
- Add a Protein: For a complete meal, stir in cooked bacon or diced ham.

NOTES _____

- "As you craft your dessert, let your spirit be playful and free. Desserts are a reminder that life's sweetest moments come when we allow ourselves to embrace joy—pour that happiness into every bite you create."

- "Baking dessert is like creating a little piece of happiness. The warmth of the oven and the sweet aromas filling the air bring comfort—let this time be your chance to indulge in the joy of treating yourself and others."

- "In every dessert, there's a sprinkle of love and a dash of joy. As you prepare your sweet creation, remember that it's not just about the taste, but the happiness and comfort it brings to those who share in its sweetness."

Desserts
Time

Peach Sorbet

2 servings   **3 hours**

INGREDIENTS

- 3 ripe peaches, peeled and chopped (about 400g)
- 2 tablespoons honey (or sugar, approx. 30ml)
- 1 tablespoon lemon juice (approx. 15ml)
- 1/4 cup water (approx. 60ml)
- Fresh mint leaves, for garnish

DIRECTIONS

1. **Prepare the peaches**: Peel and chop the peaches into small pieces.
2. **Blend the ingredients:** In a blender or food processor, combine the chopped peaches, honey, lemon juice, and water. Blend until smooth.
3. **Freeze the mixture:** Pour the peach mixture into a shallow container and place it in the freezer. Stir the mixture every 30 minutes to break up any ice crystals until it reaches a sorbet-like consistency, usually about 2-3 hours.
4. **Serve:** Once the sorbet is fully frozen and smooth, scoop it into bowls.
5. **Garnish:** Add a few fresh mint leaves on top for a refreshing touch and extra color.

Peaches: Provide natural sweetness and are rich in vitamins A and C, making this sorbet refreshing and nutritious.

Honey: Adds a natural sweetener with antibacterial properties. You can substitute with sugar if preferred.

Lemon Juice: Enhances the flavor and adds a slight tang while helping to preserve the freshness of the peaches.

Water: Helps achieve the right consistency for the sorbet.

Fresh Mint: Adds a cooling effect and fresh flavor as a garnish, enhancing the overall presentation.

Nutritional Information (Per Serving): Calories: ~100 kcal, Total Fat: 0g, Carbohydrates: 25g, Protein: 1g

"Cool down with a scoop of peach sorbet—refreshingly sweet and bursting with the essence of summer, it's a delightful treat for your taste buds!"

Serving Suggestions:

- Serve the peach sorbet as a light and refreshing dessert after a summer meal.
- The fresh mint leaves not only add visual appeal but also complement the sweetness of the sorbet.
- You can also pair it with other fruit sorbets or serve it alongside light desserts like shortbread cookies for a delightful contrast.

NOTES _____

Easy Apple Charlotte

 2 servings   40 minutes

INGREDIENTS

- 1 medium apples, peeled, cored, and sliced or cubed (approx. 150g)
- 1 large eggs or 2 small (approx. 50g)
- 1/2 cup sugar (approx. 50g)
- 1 cup flour (approx. 50 g)
- 1/4 teaspoon cinnamon (approx. 0.5g)

Optional: Vanilla extract

DIRECTIONS

1. **Prepare the apples:** Peel, core, and slice the apples into thin wedges or cubes.
2. **Prepare the batter:** In a bowl, whisk the eggs and sugar together until light and frothy. Gradually add the flour and cinnamon, stirring to form a smooth batter. You may add vanilla extract for enhancing flavor.
3. **Assemble the dessert:** In a greased baking dish, layer the apples evenly. Pour the egg batter over the apples, spreading it evenly.
4. **Bake:** Preheat the oven to 350°F (175°C) and bake the Apple Charlotte for about 30 minutes, or until golden brown and set.
5. **Serve:** Let the dish cool slightly before serving. Optionally, dust with powdered sugar or serve with whipped cream.

Apples: Provide natural sweetness and are a great source of dietary fiber, vitamin C, and antioxidants.

Eggs: Bind the ingredients together while adding protein and richness to the dessert.

Sugar: Sweetens the dish and helps caramelize the apples slightly during baking.

Flour: Creates structure for the batter and helps hold the dessert together.

Cinnamon: Adds warmth and spice, enhancing the flavor of the apples.

Nutritional Information (Per Serving): Calories: ~250 kcal, Total Fat: 4g, Carbohydrates: 48g, Protein: 5g

"Enjoy the simplicity of easy apple charlotte—layers of tender apples and soft cake come together for a delightful dessert that warms the heart!"

Serving Suggestions:
- Apple Charlotte is best served warm, either by itself or with a dollop of whipped cream or a scoop of vanilla ice cream. .
- It's a comforting dessert that works well for cozy dinners or special occasions.

NOTES _____

Classic Brownies

INGREDIENTS

- 1/4 cup all-purpose flour (approx. 30g)
- 1/4 cup unsweetened cocoa powder (approx. 25g)
- 1/2 cup sugar (approx. 100g)
- 1/4 cup butter, melted (approx. 70g)
- 1 large egg (approx. 50g)

Optional: Vanilla Extract, Chopped Nuts, Chocolate Chips

DIRECTIONS

1. **Preheat the oven** to 350°F (175°C). Grease a small baking dish or line it with parchment paper.
2. **Mix dry ingredients:** In a bowl, whisk together the flour, cocoa powder, and sugar.
3. **Add wet ingredients:** In another bowl, whisk the melted butter and egg together.
4. **Combine:** Slowly add the wet ingredients into the dry ingredients, stirring until a thick, smooth batter forms. Optional: add vanilla extract, nuts or chocolate chips.
5. **Bake:** Pour the batter into the prepared baking dish and spread it evenly. Bake for 20-25 minutes, or until a toothpick inserted into the center comes out with a few moist crumbs.
6. **Cool:** Let the brownies cool in the pan before slicing into squares.

Cocoa Powder: Gives the brownies their deep chocolate flavor.

Eggs: Bind the ingredients together while adding protein and richness to the dessert.

Sugar: Sweetens the brownies and helps create a tender texture.

Flour: Provides structure to the brownies, helping them set.

Butter: Adds richness and helps keep the brownies moist.

Nutritional Information (Per Serving): Calories: ~320 kcal, Total Fat: 16g, Carbohydrates: 43g, Protein: 4g

"Satisfy your sweet cravings with classic brownies—rich, fudgy, and a timeless treat that brings a smile with every indulgent bite!"

NOTES _____

Easy Lemon Cake

  2 servings   35 minutes

INGREDIENTS

- 1/2 cup all-purpose flour (approx. 60g)
- 1/4 cup sugar (approx. 50g)
- 1 large egg (approx. 50g)
- Zest and Juice from 1/2 a lemon
- 1/4 cup butter, melted (approx. 60g)

DIRECTIONS

1. **Preheat the oven** to 350°F (175°C) and grease a small baking dish or loaf pan.
2. **Zest the lemon:** Grate the zest from 1/2 a lemon and set aside. Cut the lemon in half and squeeze the juice (about 1 tablespoon or 15ml) into a small bowl.
3. **Whisk the eggs and sugar:** In a medium bowl, whisk the egg and sugar together until the mixture becomes pale and slightly frothy.
4. **Add butter and lemon:** Slowly whisk in the melted butter, lemon zest, and lemon juice.
- Suggestion: You may use an orange for this recipe or lemon and orange together.
5. **Add the flour:** Gradually sift the flour into the wet ingredients and stir until the batter is smooth and free of lumps.
6. **Bake:** Pour the batter into the prepared baking dish and bake for 20-25 minutes, or until a toothpick inserted into the center comes out clean.
7. **Cool:** Allow the cake to cool in the pan for a few minutes before transferring to a wire rack to cool completely.

Lemon: Provides a burst of fresh citrus flavor. Adds a tangy brightness and helps balance the sweetness.

Egg: Binds the ingredients and helps the cake rise.

Sugar: Adds sweetness and moisture.

Flour: Forms the base and gives structure to the cake.

Butter: Adds richness and tenderness to the cake.

Nutritional Information (Per Serving): Calories: ~300 kcal, Total Fat: 17g, Carbohydrates: 32g, Protein: 4g

"Brighten your day with an easy lemon cake—light, zesty, and a delightful way to bring sunshine to your dessert table!"

Serving Suggestions:
- Enjoy this lemon cake with a light dusting of powdered sugar or a drizzle of simple lemon glaze
- It pairs well with fresh berries or a cup of tea for a refreshing treat.
- The lemon zest intensifies the citrus flavor, making it perfect for lemon lovers!

NOTES _____

No-Bake Cheesecake

 2 servings   10 minutes

INGREDIENTS

- 4 ounces cream cheese, softened (approx. 113g)
- 1/4 cup sugar (approx. 50g)
- 4 graham crackers, crushed (approx. 1/2 cup crumbs or 55g)
- 2 tablespoons butter, melted (approx. 28g)
- 1/2 teaspoon vanilla extract

Optional: Berries, Fruits, Chocolate Shavings, Caramel, Fruit compote, Whipped cream

DIRECTIONS

1. **Prepare the crust:**
- Combine the crushed graham crackers with the melted butter in a small bowl, mixing until the crumbs are evenly coated.
- Press the mixture into the bottom of two small serving cups or ramekins to form the crust. Set aside.
2. **Make the cheesecake filling:**
- In a medium bowl, beat the softened cream cheese and sugar together until smooth and creamy.
- Add the vanilla extract and continue to beat until well incorporated.
3. **Assemble the cheesecake:**
- Spoon the cream cheese mixture over the prepared graham cracker crusts, spreading it evenly.
4. **Chill** the cheesecakes in the refrigerator for at least 1-2 hours, or until set.
5. **Serve:** Once chilled, you can optionally top the cheesecakes with fresh fruit, berries, chocolate shavings, caramel, fruit compote, or whipped cream before serving.

Cream Cheese: The rich, creamy base of the cheesecake, adding a smooth texture and tangy flavor.

Graham Crackers: Provide a crunchy, buttery base for the no-bake cheesecake, contrasting the creamy filling.

Sugar: Sweetens the cream cheese mixture, balancing the tanginess.

Vanilla Extract: Adds a delicate flavor that enhances the cream cheese and balances the sweetness.

Butter: Binds the graham cracker crumbs together and adds richness to the crust.

Nutritional Information (Per Serving): Calories: ~300 kcal, Total Fat: 22g, Carbohydrates: 30g, Protein: 4g

"Treat yourself to the lusciousness of no-bake cheesecake—velvety smooth and refreshingly easy, it's a dessert that brings joy without the fuss!"

Serving Suggestions:
- Serve these no-bake cheesecakes chilled for a refreshing dessert.
- Top with fresh berries, chocolate shavings, or a drizzle of caramel for an extra touch of flavor.
- These mini cheesecakes are perfect for individual servings, making them ideal for dinner parties or small gatherings.

NOTES _____

Yogurt and Fruit Dip

 2 servings 5 minutes

INGREDIENTS

- 1/2 cup Greek yogurt (approx. 120g)
- 1 tablespoon honey (approx. 15g)
- 1/2 cup fresh fruit (e.g., strawberries, raspberries, blueberries, banana, apple slices, ananas, watermelon) (approx. 75g)
- 1/4 teaspoon cinnamon
- 2 tablespoons almonds (or other nuts), chopped (approx. 15g)

DIRECTIONS

1. **Prepare the dip:**
- In a small bowl, mix the Greek yogurt, honey, and cinnamon until well combined.
2. **Add fruit and almonds:**
- Arrange the fresh fruit around the yogurt dip in a serving bowl.
- Sprinkle the chopped almonds (or other nuts) on top of the yogurt for a bit of crunch.
3. **Serve:**
- Serve the yogurt dip immediately with fresh fruit for dipping. You can refrigerate it for 10-15 minutes if you prefer a cooler dip.

Greek Yogurt: Provides creaminess, protein, and probiotics, making the dip thick and tangy.

Honey: Sweetens the yogurt naturally while also adding a smooth texture.

Fresh Fruit: Strawberries or other fresh fruit provide a burst of natural sweetness and a juicy texture.

Cinnamon: Adds warmth and a slight spice that complements the sweetness of the honey and fruit.

Almonds: Add a satisfying crunch and a nutty flavor that balances the creamy dip.

Nutritional Information (Per Serving): Calories: ~170 kcal, Total Fat: 6g, Carbohydrates: 24g, Protein: 7g

"Dip into the creamy goodness of yogurt and fruit—light, refreshing, and a naturally sweet way to satisfy your dessert cravings with a healthy twist!"

Serving Suggestions:
- This yogurt and fruit dip is perfect for a quick snack, a healthy breakfast, or a light dessert.
- Serve it with a variety of fresh fruits like apple slices, grapes, or blueberries for a colorful, nutritious platter. The combination of sweet, tangy, and crunchy flavors makes this dip a crowd-pleaser!

NOTES _____

Poached Pears with Chocolate

  2 servings 40 minutes

INGREDIENTS

- 2 ripe pears (approx. 300g total)
- 1 cup red wine (or water) (approx. 240ml)
- 1/2 cup sugar (approx. 100g)
- 1 teaspoon vanilla extract (approx. 5ml)
- 1/4 cup dark chocolate, chopped (approx. 40g)

Optional: fresh mint leaves, sea salt, nuts

DIRECTIONS

1. **Prepare the Pears:** Wash and Peel the pears, leaving the stems intact. You can also slice a small amount off the bottom to help them stand upright.
2. **Poach the Pears:** In a saucepan, combine red wine (or water), sugar, and vanilla extract. Bring to a simmer over medium heat, stirring until the sugar dissolves. Add the pears and simmer for 20-25 minutes, turning occasionally, until the pears are tender but not mushy. You can add more wine or water if needed.
3. **Make the Chocolate Sauce:** While the pears are poaching, melt the dark chocolate in a heatproof bowl over a pot of simmering water (double boiler method) or in the microwave in 30-second intervals, stirring until smooth.
4. **Serve:** Once the pears are done, remove them from the poaching liquid and place them on serving plates. Drizzle with the melted chocolate sauce.
5. **Garnish (Optional):** You can garnish with fresh mint leaves or a sprinkle of sea salt or nuts for added flavor.

Pears: A naturally sweet and juicy fruit that serves as the base of the dish, providing vitamins and fiber.

Red Wine: Adds rich flavor and helps to tenderize the pears during poaching.

Sugar: Sweetens the poaching liquid and balances the acidity of the wine.

Vanilla Extract: Enhances the flavor profile with its aromatic qualities.

Dark Chocolate: Rich in antioxidants, it adds a decadent touch and depth of flavor.

Nutritional Information (Per Serving): Calories: ~350 kcal, Total Fat: 6g, Carbohydrates: 67g, Protein: 2g

"Delight in the elegance of poached pears with chocolate—tender, luscious, and a decadent way to indulge in a sweet, sophisticated dessert!"

Serving Suggestions:
- Serve the poached pears warm or chilled, drizzled with the chocolate sauce.
- They can be accompanied by a scoop of vanilla ice cream or a dollop of whipped cream for a delightful dessert. Enjoy with a glass of dessert wine for a complete experience.

NOTES _____

Eton Mess

🍴 2 servings   🕐 10 minutes

INGREDIENTS

- 1 cup heavy cream (approx. 240ml)
- 2 tablespoons powdered sugar (approx. 15g)
- 1 cup mixed berries (e.g., strawberries, raspberries, blueberries) (approx. 150g)
- 2 meringue nests (store-bought or homemade)
- 1 teaspoon vanilla extract (approx. 5ml)

DIRECTIONS

1. **Prepare the Cream:** In a mixing bowl, whip the heavy cream with powdered sugar and vanilla extract until soft peaks form.
2. **Prepare the Berries:** If using strawberries, hull and slice them. Take a half of sliced strawberries and meshed them in a small bowl with a folk. Mix all the berries and meshed strawberries together in a bowl.
3. **Crush the Meringues:** Lightly crush the meringue nests into bite-sized pieces.
4. **Assemble the Eton Mess:** In serving glasses or bowls, layer the whipped cream, mixed berries, and crushed meringue. Repeat the layers until the glasses are filled.
5. **Garnish (Optional):** Top with a few whole berries or a sprig of mint for presentation.

Heavy Cream: Provides richness and a creamy texture, making it the base of the dessert.

Powdered Sugar: Sweetens the cream, allowing for a smooth consistency without grittiness.

Mixed Berries: Adds freshness, natural sweetness, and vibrant color, as well as antioxidants and vitamins.

Meringue Nests: Contributes a light, crunchy texture that contrasts beautifully with the cream and berries.

Vanilla Extract: Enhances the overall flavor of the dish with a warm, aromatic note.

Nutritional Information (Per Serving): Calories: ~300 kcal, Total Fat: 18g, Carbohydrates: 30g, Protein: 3g

"Savor the delightful chaos of Eton Mess—a luscious combination of crushed meringue, whipped cream, and fresh berries that brings a playful twist to your dessert experience!"

Serving Suggestions:
- Eton Mess is best served immediately after assembling to retain the crunch of the meringue.
- It makes for a delightful dessert for summer gatherings or picnics.
- You can also customize it by using different seasonal fruits or flavored whipped cream for variation.

NOTES _____

Chocolate Cream

2 servings   40 minutes

INGREDIENTS

- 1 cup milk (approx. 240ml)
- 2 tablespoons cocoa powder (approx. 15g)
- 2 tablespoons sugar (approx. 25g)
- 2 tablespoons all-purpose flour (approx. 16g)
- 2 tablespoons butter (approx. 28g)

Optional: fresh mint leaves, nuts, chocolate shavings

DIRECTIONS

1. **Mix Dry Ingredients:** In a medium bowl, whisk together the cocoa powder, sugar, and flour until well combined.
2. **Combine with Milk:** Gradually add the milk to the dry ingredients, whisking continuously to prevent lumps from forming.
3. **Heat the Mixture:** Pour the mixture into a saucepan over medium heat. Cook, stirring constantly until the mixture thickens and starts to bubble. This should take about 5–7 minutes.
4. **Add Butter:** Once thickened, remove from heat and stir in the butter until fully melted and combined.
5. **Cool:** Transfer the chocolate cream to serving dishes or bowls. Let it cool at room temperature, then refrigerate for at least 30 minutes to firm up.
6. **Serve:** Serve chilled as a dessert on its own or as a filling for pastries, tarts, or cakes. Optionally top with a few whole berries, chocolate shavings or fresh mint leaves for presentation.

Milk: Provides creaminess and is the base for the chocolate cream.

Cocoa Powder: Gives the chocolate flavor and rich color to the cream.

Sugar: Sweetens the cream, balancing the bitterness of cocoa.

Flour: Acts as a thickening agent to give the cream a smooth and rich texture.

Butter: Adds richness and a silky mouthfeel to the chocolate cream.

Nutritional Information (Per Serving): Calories: ~210 kcal, Total Fat: 12g, Carbohydrates: 23g, Protein: 5g

"Indulge in the velvety richness of chocolate cream—a luscious treat that melts in your mouth, perfect for elevating any dessert or enjoying on its own!"

Serving Suggestions:
- Chocolate cream can be served on its own in dessert cups, topped with whipped cream, or garnished with chocolate shavings.
- It can also be used as a filling for cream puffs, éclairs, or layered in cakes.
- Pair with fresh fruit or a drizzle of chocolate sauce for an extra treat. Enjoy!

NOTES _____

Coconut Kisses

🍴 2 servings   🕐 30 minutes

INGREDIENTS

- 1 1/2 cup shredded coconut (approx. 100g)
- 1 large egg
- 1/4 cup sugar (approx. 50g)
- 1/4 teaspoon vanilla extract
- 1 oz dark chocolate (optional, for decoration)

DIRECTIONS

1. **Preheat the Oven:** Preheat your oven to 325°F (160°C) and line a baking sheet with parchment paper.
2. **Prepare the Mixture:** In a mixing bowl, whisk together the egg and sugar until well combined and slightly frothy.
3. **Add the Coconut:** Stir in the shredded coconut and vanilla extract. Mix thoroughly until the coconut is well coated with the egg-sugar mixture.
4. **Rest the Mixture:** If you have time, let the mixture sit for 15 minutes to allow the shredded coconut to soften and absorb the liquid. This step ensures a more tender texture.
5. **Form the Kisses:** Using your hands or a small cookie scoop, form small balls (about 1 tablespoon each) from the coconut mixture and place them on the prepared baking sheet.
6. **Bake:** Bake for 12-15 minutes or until the edges are golden brown and the tops are slightly crisp.
7. **Optional Chocolate Decoration:** If you'd like to decorate with chocolate, melt the dark chocolate in a microwave-safe bowl in 20-second intervals, stirring in between. Drizzle the melted chocolate over the baked coconut kisses or dip the bottom of each kiss into the chocolate. Let the chocolate set before serving.
8. **Serve:** Let the coconut kisses cool completely on the baking sheet before serving.

Coconut: The main ingredient, adding texture, flavor, and healthy fats. It provides a tropical sweetness and chewy texture.

Sugar: Adds sweetness and helps create a slight caramelization on the outside of the kisses.

Egg: Binds the coconut mixture together and gives the kisses their structure.

Vanilla Extract: Enhances the flavor with a hint of warmth.

Chocolate (optional): Adds a delightful contrast of bitter (dark chocolate) or sweet (white chocolate) flavors to the coconut.

Nutritional Information (Per Serving): Calories: ~230 kcal, Total Fat: 14g, Carbohydrates: 22g, Protein: 3g

"Enjoy the tropical sweetness of coconut kisses—bite-sized, chewy delights that bring the perfect balance of coconut flavor and sugary bliss!"

Serving Suggestions:
- These coconut kisses make for a delightful treat on their own but can be elevated with a drizzle of melted dark or white chocolate for added indulgence.
- Perfect for tea-time snacks, holiday trays, or dessert bites, they are versatile and crowd-pleasing!
- You can also sprinkle some extra coconut on top for decoration before the chocolate drizzle sets.

NOTES _____

Fruits with Chocolate Dip

 2 servings 10 minutes

INGREDIENTS

- 1/2 cup dark chocolate chips (approx. 85g)
- 1/4 cup heavy cream (approx. 60ml)
- 1 tablespoon honey (optional, for added sweetness)
- 1 teaspoon vanilla extract
- Assorted fresh fruits (e.g., strawberries, banana slices, apple wedges, pineapple chunks)

DIRECTIONS

1. **Prepare the Fruits:** Wash and cut your chosen fruits into bite-sized pieces or slices. Arrange them on a serving platter.
2. **Melt the Chocolate:** In a microwave-safe bowl, combine the dark chocolate chips and heavy cream. Heat in the microwave in 20-second intervals, stirring after each interval, until the chocolate is fully melted and smooth. Be careful not to overheat the chocolate.
3. **Add Honey and Vanilla (Optional):** Once the chocolate is smooth, stir in the honey (if using) and vanilla extract for extra flavor.
4. **Serve:** Pour the chocolate dip into a small serving bowl and place it on the platter alongside the fruits. Dip the fruits into the chocolate and enjoy!

Fruits: Fresh fruits like strawberries, bananas, and apples offer a refreshing contrast to the rich chocolate, with natural sweetness and a variety of textures.

Dark Chocolate Chips: Provide a rich, indulgent flavor with a hint of bitterness, balancing the sweetness of the fruits.

Heavy Cream: Adds smoothness and richness to the chocolate, creating a creamy dip texture.

Vanilla Extract: Enhances the flavor of the chocolate, adding a sweet, aromatic touch.

Honey (Optional): Adds natural sweetness to the chocolate dip.

Nutritional Information (Per Serving): Calories: ~250 kcal, Total Fat: 17g, Carbohydrates: 22g, Protein: 2g

"Indulge in the sweet harmony of fruits and chocolate dip—a playful balance of fresh and rich flavors that makes every bite feel like a little celebration!"

Serving Suggestions:
- You can experiment with different fruits like grapes, oranges, or kiwi for more variety.
- For a fun twist, consider adding marshmallows, pretzels, or graham crackers as additional dippers.
- To make this dessert more interactive, set up a fondue station where guests can dip their own fruit into the chocolate!

NOTES _____

NOTES

Made in the USA
Las Vegas, NV
16 December 2024

14355741R00083